SECOND EDITION

TOP NOTCH

English for Today's World

WITH WORKBOOK

Joan Saslow • Allen Ascher

With *Top Notch Pop Songs and Karaoke*
by Rob Morsberger

Top Notch: English for Today's World 1A with Workbook, Second Edition

Pearson Education, 10 Bank Street, White Plains, NY 10606

Staff credits: The people who made up the *Top Notch 1* team—representing editorial, design, production, and manufacturing—are Rhea Banker, Elizabeth Carlson, Aerin Csigay, Dave Dickey, Warren Fischbach, Aliza Greenblatt, Ray Keating, Mike Kemper, Barbara Sabella, and Martin Yu.

Cover design: Rhea Banker
Cover photo: Sprint/Corbis
Text design: Elizabeth Carlson and Wendy Wolf
Text composition: Quarasan!
Text font: 9/10 Stone Sans, ITC Stone Sans

Library of Congress Cataloging-in-Publication Data

Saslow, Joan M.
Top notch : English for today's world / Joan Saslow, Allen Ascher ; with Top Notch pop songs and Karaoke by Rob Morsberger. — 2nd ed.
p. cm.
ISBN 0-13-246988-X (set) — ISBN 0-13-247038-1 (v. 1) — ISBN 0-13-247048-9 (v. 2) — ISBN 0-13-247027-6 (v. 3) 1. English language — Textbooks for foreign speakers. 2. English language — Problems, exercises, etc. I. Ascher, Allen. II. Title.
PE1128.S2757 2011
428.2'4 — dc22
2010019162

ISBN 13: 978-0-13-247039-1
ISBN 10: 0-13-247039-X

Photo credits: All original photography by Michal Heron and Sharon Hoogstraten. Page 2 (background) Shutterstock.com, (top left) Michael S. Yamashita/Corbis, (middle) Jose Luis Pelaez, Inc./Corbis, (right) Peter Turnley/Corbis, (bottom left) Ariel Skelley/Corbis; p. 3 (bottom left) Bryan Bedder/Getty Images, (bottom right) LAN/Corbis; p. 5 (top) Shutterstock.com; p. 6 (left) Jason Merritt/Getty Images; p. 7 (top left) AP Images/Chris Pizzello, (top right) Kevin Mazur/Getty Images, (bottom) AP Images/Stephen Chernin; p. 9 (top left) Shutterstock.com, (top right) Shutterstock.com, (middle left) Shutterstock.com, (middle right) Shutterstock.com; p. 11 (right) Shutterstock.com; p. 12 Shutterstock.com; p. 13 (top right) AP Images/Diane Bondareff, (middle) iStockphoto.com, (bottom) Shutterstock.com, (bottom background) Shutterstock.com; p. 15 Dorling Kindersley; p. 21 (top middle) Peter Klaunzer/Corbis, (top right) Jo Hale/Getty Images, (bottom middle) Scala/Art Resource, NY, (bottom right) Vincent West/Reuters/Corbis; p. 22 (top left) Shutterstock.com; p. 25 (background) Shutterstock.com; p. 26 (grandparents) Lindy Powers/Index Stock Imagery, (Linda) Shutterstock.com, (uncle, aunt, cousins) Getty Images, (parents) Ryan McVay/Getty Images, (mother-in-law) Ron Chapple/Getty Images, (father-in-law) James Darell/Getty Images, (sister-in-law, brother, nephew, niece) Royalty-Free/Corbis, (sister) Cleve Bryant/PhotoEdit, (children) Shutterstock.com, (brother-in-law) Bill Cannon/Getty Images; p. 30 (top left) Jerome Tisne/Getty Images, (top middle) Mel Yates/Getty Images, (top right) Astock/Corbis, (bottom left) Andersen Ross/Jupiterimages, (bottom middle) Terry Vine/Corbis, (bottom right) Photos.com; p. 37 (background) Shutterstock.com, (Enrique) Alexander Tamargo/Getty Images, (Ronna) Europa Press/Gamma/eyedea/picturedesk.com, (Dr. Julio) Europa Press/Gamma/eyedea/picturedesk.com, (Miranda) Torra Terry/Gamma/eyedea/picturedesk.com, (Julio) Robert Duyos/AFP/Getty Images, (Isabel P.) Carlos Alvarez/Getty Images, (Guillermo) Europa Press/Gamma/eyedea/picturedesk.com, (Victoria) Europa Press/Gamma/eyedea/picturedesk.com, (Cristina) Europa Press/Gamma/eyedea/picturedesk.com, (Rodrigo) Europa Press/Gamma/eyedea/picturedesk.com, (Miguel) Europa Press/Gamma/eyedea/picturedesk.com, (Isabel) Alexander Tamargo/Getty Images, (Julio) Stephane Cardinale/People Avenue/Corbis, (Enrique) Alexander Tamargo/Getty Images; p. 38 (top left) Shutterstock.com, (potato soup) Jupiterimages/Getty Images, (fried squid) iStockphoto.com, (tomato onion) Image Source/PictureQuest-Royalty Free, (fish) Colin Cooke/Getty Images, (chicken) Tom Vano/Jupiterimages, (cake) Francisco Cruz/SuperStock; p. 41 (sandwich) iStockphoto.com; p. 46 (top right) C Squared Studios/Getty Images, (left) Shutterstock.com, (middle) Amy Etra/PhotoEdit Inc., (right) Shutterstock.com; p. 49 (background) iStockphoto.com, (1) Comstock Images/Getty Images, (2) Jacobs Stock Photography/Getty Images, (3) Jochen Sand/Getty Images, (4) iStockphoto.com, (salad) Shutterstock.com, (pasta) Shutterstock.com, (fish) Dorling Kindersley, (shrimp) Dorling Kindersley; p. 50 (laptop) Shutterstock.com, (desktop) Shutterstock.com, (earphone) Shutterstock.com, (gps) Shutterstock.com, (dvd) iStockphoto.com, (flash) Shutterstock.com, (camera) courtesy Canon USA, (headphones) Shutterstock.com, (earbuds) Shutterstock.com, (projector) iStockphoto.com, (mp3) iStockphoto.com, (camcorder) Shutterstock.com, (speakers) Logitech, Inc.; p. 82 (tv) Shutterstock.com; p. 53 (smart) Shutterstock.com, (cell) Nokia, (scanner) iStockphoto.com, (photocopier) Getty Images, (fax) EyeWire Collection/Getty Images; p. 54 (top right) Anthony Meshkinyar/Getty Images, (2) Silver Burdett Ginn, (3) Melba Photo Agency/PunchStock, (4) Shutterstock.com, (5) Dorling Kindersley, (6) Shutterstock.com, (7) Shutterstock.com, (8) Piotr Maslej, (10) Shutterstock.com, (11) Will Crocker/Getty Images, (13) iStockphoto.com, (14) Peter Holmes/Photolibrary, (16) Photos.com, (17) Shutterstock.com; p. 56 (top) Shutterstock.com, (left) Shutterstock.com, (middle) Shutterstock.com, (right) Shutterstock.com; p. 61 (background) Mikael Dubois/Getty Images, (1) iStockphoto.com and Shutterstock.com, (2) Jim Corwin/Getty Images, (middle) iStockphoto.com, (3) PhotosIndia/Getty Images and Shutterstock.com, (4 left) Shutterstock.com, (4 middle) Hitoshi Nishimura/Getty Images, (4 right) Shutterstock.com; p. W7 Shutterstock; p. W9 Bryan Bedder/Getty Images; p. W11 (left) Frank Micelotta/Getty Images, (middle left) Jason Fulford, photo courtesy of American International Artists, (middle right) Tim Mosenfelder/Corbis, (right) Hulton-Deutsch collection/Corbis; p. W16 (left) Shutterstock; p. W17 Randy Taylor/Index Stock Imagery; p. W21 (left) Ryan McVay/Getty Images, (middle) Cleve Bryant/PhotoEdit Inc., (right) Royalty-Free/Corbis; p. W27 Shutterstock; p. W30 Nathaniel S. Butler/NBAE/Getty Images; p. W46 Dorling Kindersley; p. W49 Shutterstock.

Illustration credits: Steve Attoe, pp. W46, W47; Kenneth Batelman, p. 40; Bob Doucet, p. 25; Leanne Franson, p. W4; Scott Fray, p. 47; Michael A. Hill, p. 19; Brian Hughes, pp. 53, W13; Stephen Hutchings, pp. W3, W31, W33, W35; Poul Lange, p. 41; Pat Lewis, p. 28; Andy Meyer, pp. 8, 57; Sandy Nichols, p. 24; Janet Norquist, p. 18; NSV Productions, pp. W32, W42, W39, W41; Dusan Petricic, pp. 17, 42, 43, W22; Michel Rabagliati, p. W25; Phil Scheuer, pp. 21 (top), 58; Steven Stankiewicz, p. 20; Anna Vltfort, p. 21.

Printed in the United States of America
2 3 4 5 6 7 8 9 10 – V042 – 15 14 13 12 11

CONTENTS

Learning Objectives

Top Notch 1 learning objectives are designed for false beginners. They offer a rigorous review and an expansion of key beginning concepts as well as a wealth of new and challenging material.

Unit	Communication Goals	Vocabulary	Grammar
1 **Getting Acquainted** page 2	• Meet someone new • Identify and describe people • Provide personal information • Introduce someone to a group	• Usage of formal titles • Positive adjectives to describe people • Personal information • Countries and nationalities	• Information questions with be (review and common errors) • Modification with adjectives (review) • Yes / no questions and short answers with be (review) **GRAMMAR BOOSTER** • Be: usage and form (review) • Be: common errors • Possessive nouns and adjectives (review)
2 **Going Out** page 14	• Accept or decline an invitation • Express locations and give directions • Make plans to see an event • Talk about musical tastes	• Music genres • Entertainment and cultural events • Locations and directions	• Prepositions of time and place • Questions with When, What time, and Where (review) **GRAMMAR BOOSTER** • Prepositions of time and place: usage
3 **The Extended Family** page 26	• Report news about relationships • Describe extended families • Compare people • Discuss family cultural traditions	• Extended family relationships • Marital status • Relatives by marriage • Describing similarities and differences	• The simple present tense (review): ◦ Affirmative and negative statements ◦ Yes / no questions ◦ Information questions ◦ Common errors **GRAMMAR BOOSTER** • The simple present tense: ◦ Usage, form, common errors ◦ Questions with Who
4 **Food and Restaurants** page 38	• Ask for a restaurant recommendation • Order from a menu • Speak to a server and pay for a meal • Discuss food and health	• Parts of a meal • Categories of food and drink • Communicating with a waiter or waitress • Adjectives to describe the healthfulness of food	• There is and there are with count and non-count nouns • Anything and nothing: common errors • Definite article the: usage **GRAMMAR BOOSTER** • Non-count nouns: usage, expressing quantities • How much / How many • Count nouns: Spelling rules • Some and any
5 **Technology and You** page 50	• Suggest a brand or model • Express frustration and sympathy • Describe features of products • Complain when things don't work	• Electronic products • Household appliances and machines • Features of manufactured products • Ways to state a problem • Ways to sympathize • Positive and negative adjectives	• The present continuous (review): ◦ Actions in progress and future plans ◦ Statements and questions **GRAMMAR BOOSTER** • The present continuous: form and spelling rules

Conversation Strategies	Listening/ Pronunciation	Reading	Writing
• Begin responses with a question to confirm • Use Let's to suggest a course of action • Ask personal questions to indicate friendliness • Intensify an informal answer with sure	**Listening Skills:** • Listen for details • Infer information **Pronunciation:** • Intonation of questions	**Texts:** • An enrollment form • Personal profiles • A photo story **Skills/strategies:** • Infer information • Scan for facts	**Task:** • Write a description of a classmate **WRITING BOOSTER** • Capitalization
• Use Really? to express enthusiasm • Provide reasons to decline an invitation • Use Too bad to express disappointment • Repeat with rising intonation to confirm information • Use Thanks, anyway to acknowledge an unsuccessful attempt to help	**Listening Skills:** • Infer a speaker's intention • Listen for main ideas • Listen for details • Listen for locations **Pronunciation:** • Rising intonation to confirm information	**Texts:** • A music website • An entertainment events page • Authentic interviews • A survey of musical tastes • A photo story **Skills/strategies:** • Interpret maps and diagrams • Identify supporting details • Make personal comparisons	**Task:** • Write a short personal essay about one's musical tastes **WRITING BOOSTER** • The sentence
• Use Actually to introduce a topic • Respond to good news with Congratulations! • Respond to bad news with I'm sorry to hear that • Use Thanks for asking to acknowledge an inquiry of concern • Use Well to introduce a lengthy reply • Ask follow-up questions to keep a conversation going	**Listening Skills:** • Infer information • Understand key details • Identify similarities and differences • Listen to take notes • Listen for main ideas • Listen for details **Pronunciation:** • Blending sounds	**Texts:** • Family tree diagrams • A self-help website • A cultural-information survey • A photo story **Skills/strategies:** • Interpret a diagram • Confirm facts • Infer information	**Task:** • Make a Venn diagram • Compare two people in a family **WRITING BOOSTER** • Combining sentences with and or but
• Use Could you ...? to make a polite request • Use Sure to agree to a request • Clarify a request by asking for more specific information • Indicate a sudden thought with Actually • Use I'll have to order from a server • Increase politeness with please	**Listening Skills:** • Listen to take notes • Infer the location of a conversation • Listen to predict **Pronunciation:** • The before consonant and vowel sounds	**Texts:** • Menus • A nutrition website • A photo story **Skills/strategies:** • Interpret a map • Understand from context • Infer information	**Task:** • Write a short article about food for a travel newsletter **WRITING BOOSTER** • Connecting words and ideas: and, in addition
• Use Hey or How's it going for an informal greeting • Use What about...? to offer a suggestion • Use Really? to indicate surprise • Use You know to introduce a topic • Express sympathy when someone is frustrated	**Listening Skills:** • Listen to predict • Infer meaning • Listen for details **Pronunciation:** • Intonation of questions	**Texts:** • Newspaper advertisements • A magazine ad for a new product • A photo story **Skills/strategies:** • Understand from context • Activate language from a text	**Task:** • Write a paragraph describing a product **WRITING BOOSTER** • Placement of adjectives

Conversation Strategies	Listening/ Pronunciation	Reading	Writing
• Use Why don't we . . . ? to suggest an activity • Say Sorry, I can't to apologize for turning down an invitation • Provide a reason with have to to decline an invitation • Use Well, how about . . . ? to suggest an alternative • Use How come? to ask for a reason • Use a negative question to confirm information	**Listening Skills:** • Infer meaning • Infer information • Listen for main ideas • Listen for details • Apply and personalize information **Pronunciation:** • Can / can't • The third-person singular -s	**Texts:** • A bar graph • A fitness survey • A magazine article • A photo story **Skills/strategies:** • Interpret a bar graph • Infer information • Summarize	**Task:** • Write an interview about health and exercise habits **WRITING BOOSTER** • Punctuation of statements and questions
• Say Welcome back! to indicate enthusiasm about someone's return from a trip • Acknowledge someone's interest with Actually • Decline an offer of assistance with That's OK. I'm fine. • Confirm that an offer is declined with Are you sure? • Use Absolutely to confirm a response • Show enthusiasm with No kidding! and Tell me more	**Listening Skills:** • Listen for main ideas • Listen for details • Infer meaning **Pronunciation:** • The simple past tense ending: regular verbs	**Texts:** • Travel brochures • Personal travel stories • A vacation survey • A photo story **Skills/strategies:** • Activate language from a text • Draw conclusions • Identify supporting details	**Task:** • Write a guided essay about a vacation **WRITING BOOSTER** • Time order
• Use Excuse me to indicate you didn't understand or couldn't hear • Use Excuse me to begin a conversation with a clerk • Follow a question with more information for clarification • Acknowledge someone's assistance with Thanks for your help • Respond to gratitude with My pleasure	**Listening Skills:** • Infer the appropriate location • Infer the locations of conversations • Understand locations and directions **Pronunciation:** • Contrastive stress for clarification	**Texts:** • A clothing catalogue • Simple and complex diagrams and plans • A travel blog • A personal opinion survey • A photo story **Skills/strategies:** • Paraphrase • Identify supporting details • Apply information	**Task:** • Write an e-mail or letter explaining what clothes to pack **WRITING BOOSTER** • Connecting ideas with because and since
• Use I'm sorry to respond with disappointing information • Use Well to introduce an alternative. • Use I hope so to politely respond to an offer of help • Use Let me check to buy time to get information	**Listening Skills:** • Infer the type of travel service • Understand public announcements • Listen for details • Use reasoning to evaluate statements of fact **Pronunciation:** • Intonation for stating alternatives	**Texts:** • Transportation schedules • Public transportation tickets • Arrival and departure boards • Newspaper articles • A photo story **Skills/strategies:** • Make decisions based on schedules and needs • Critical thinking	**Task:** • Write two paragraphs about trips **WRITING BOOSTER** • The paragraph
• Use Well to connect an answer to an earlier question • Use How about . . .? to make a financial offer • Use OK to indicate that an agreement has been reached	**Listening Skills:** • Listen for details • Listen for main ideas **Pronunciation:** • Rising intonation for clarification	**Texts:** • A travel guide • A magazine article • Personal travel stories • A photo story **Skills/strategies:** • Draw conclusions • Apply information	**Task:** • Write a guide to your city, including information on where to stay, visit, and shop **WRITING BOOSTER** • Connecting contradictory ideas: even though, however, on the other hand

To the Teacher

What is *Top Notch*?

Top Notch is a six-level* communicative course that prepares adults and young adults to interact successfully and confidently with both native and non-native speakers of English.

The goal of the *Top Notch* course is to make English unforgettable through:

- Multiple exposures to new language
- Numerous opportunities to practice it
- Deliberate and intensive recycling

The *Top Notch* course has two beginning levels: *Top Notch* Fundamentals for true beginners and *Top Notch* 1 for false beginners.

Each full level of *Top Notch* contains enough material for 60 to 90 hours of classroom instruction. A wide choice of supplementary components makes it easy to tailor *Top Notch* to the needs of your classes.

******Summit* 1 and *Summit* 2 are the titles of the fifth and sixth levels of the *Top Notch* course. All Student's Books are available in split editions with bound-in workbooks.**

The *Top Notch* instructional design

Daily confirmation of progress

Each easy-to-follow two-page lesson begins with a clearly stated communication goal. All lesson activities are integrated with the goal and systematically build toward a final speaking activity in which students demonstrate achievement of the goal. "Can-do" statements in each unit ensure students' awareness of the continuum of their progress.

A purposeful conversation syllabus

Memorable conversation models provide essential and practical social language that students can carry "in their pockets" for use in real life. Guided conversation pair work enables students to modify, personalize, and extend each model so they can use it to communicate their <u>own</u> thoughts and needs. Free discussion activities are carefully crafted so students can continually retrieve and use the language from the models. All conversation models are informed by the Longman Corpus of Spoken American English.

An emphasis on cultural fluency

Recognizing that English is a global language, *Top Notch* actively equips students to interact socially with people from a variety of cultures and deliberately prepares them to understand accented speakers from diverse language backgrounds.

Intensive vocabulary development

Students actively work with a rich vocabulary of high-frequency words, collocations, and expressions in all units of the Student's Book. Clear illustrations and definitions clarify meaning and provide support for independent study, review, and test preparation. Systematic recycling promotes smooth and continued acquisition of vocabulary from the beginning to the advanced levels of the course.

A dynamic approach to grammar

An explicit grammar syllabus is supported by charts containing clear grammar rules, relevant examples, and explanations of meaning and use. Numerous grammar exercises provide focused practice, and grammar usage is continually activated in communication exercises that illustrate the grammar being learned.

A dedicated pronunciation syllabus

Focused pronunciation, rhythm, and intonation practice is included in each unit, providing application of each pronunciation point to the target language of the unit and facilitating comprehensible pronunciation.

ActiveBook

SECOND EDITION
TOP NOTCH 1
with ActiveBook

Top Notch

Top Notch 1 ActiveBook

Contents
More Practice

Learning Objectives
Unit 1: Getting Acquainted
Unit 2: Going Out
Unit 3: The Extended Family
Unit 4: Food and Restaurants
Unit 5: Technology and You
Unit 6: Staying in Shape
Unit 7: On Vacation
Unit 8: Shopping for Clothes
Unit 9: Taking Transportation
Unit 10: Shopping Smart
Reference Charts
Grammar Booster
Writing Booster
Top Notch Pop Lyrics

A Digital Student's Book
(with complete audio)

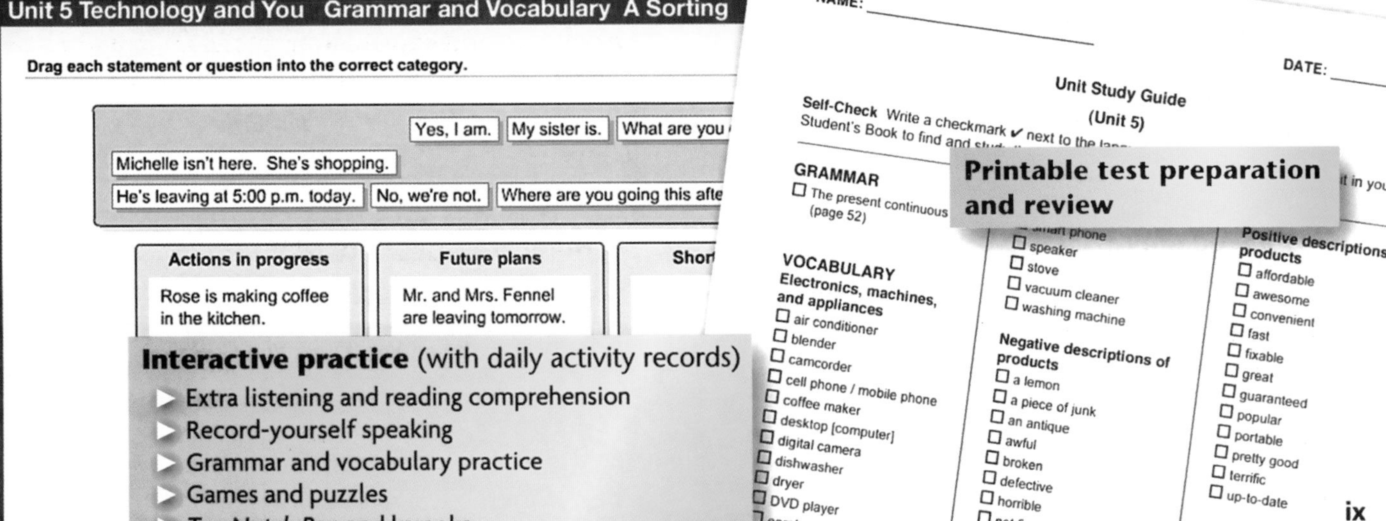

The Teacher's Edition and Lesson Planner

Includes:

- A bound-in Methods Handbook for professional development
- Detailed lesson plans with suggested teaching times
- Language, culture, and corpus notes
- Student's Book and Workbook answer keys
- Audioscripts
- *Top Notch TV* teaching notes
- **ActiveTeach**
  - A Digital Student's Book with interactive whiteboard (IWB) software
  - Instantly accessible audio and *Top Notch TV* video
  - Interactive exercises from the Student's *ActiveBook* for in-class use
  - A complete menu of printable extension activities

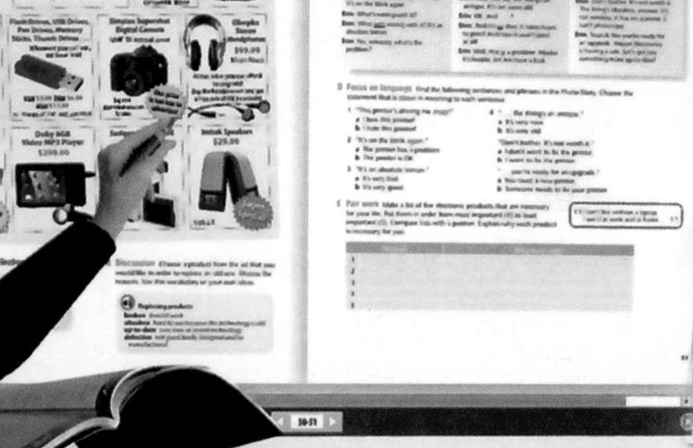

Top Notch TV

A hilarious situation comedy, authentic unrehearsed on-the-street interviews, and *Top Notch Pop* karaoke.

The Digital Student's Book

With zoom, write, highlight, save and other IWB tools.

Printable Extension Activities

Including:

- Writing process worksheets
- Vocabulary flashcards
- Learning strategies
- Graphic organizers
- Pronunciation activities
- Video activity worksheets and more . . .

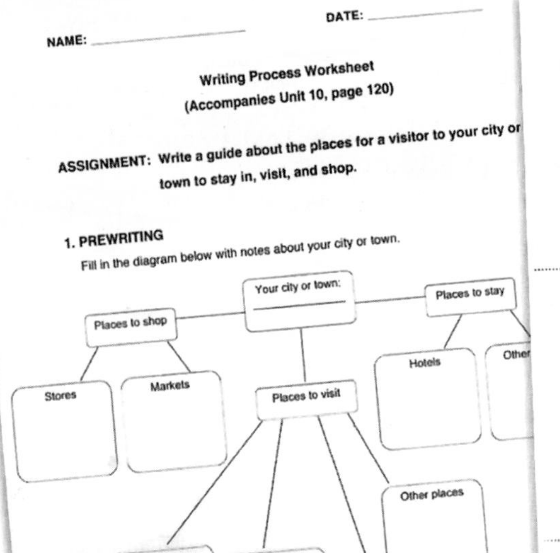

Page 1 of 2

NAME: ______________ DATE: ______________

Writing Process Worksheet
(Accompanies Unit 10, page 120)

ASSIGNMENT: Write a guide about the places for a visitor to your city or town to stay in, visit, and shop.

1. PREWRITING
Fill in the diagram below with notes about your city or town.

Electronics

Electronics

NAME: ______________

Learning Strategy
(Unit 6, page 70, Reading)

READING STRATEGY: skimming

When you read an article, skim for the main ideas first before you read for details.

In the article below, the unimportant parts have been deleted. Notice how much you can understand with fewer words in the article.

When You Think You Can't . . .

Mark Zupan

Bethany Hamilton

Other components

Workbook

Daily assignments that reinforce each lesson.

Classroom Audio Program

Includes a variety of authentic regional and non-native accents.

Complete Assessment Package

Ready-made achievement tests. Software provides option to edit, delete, or add items.

Full-Course Placement Tests

Choose printable or online version.

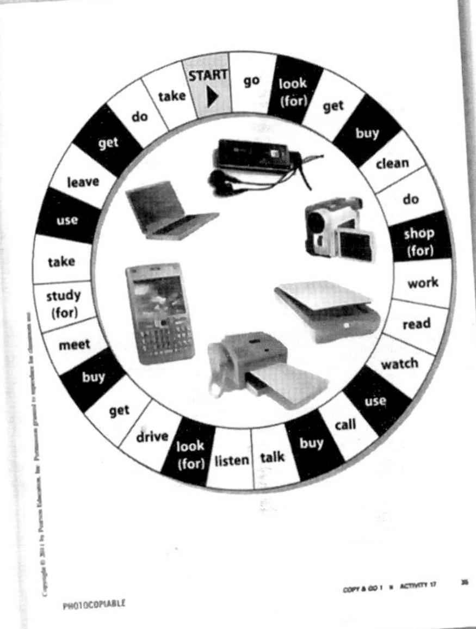

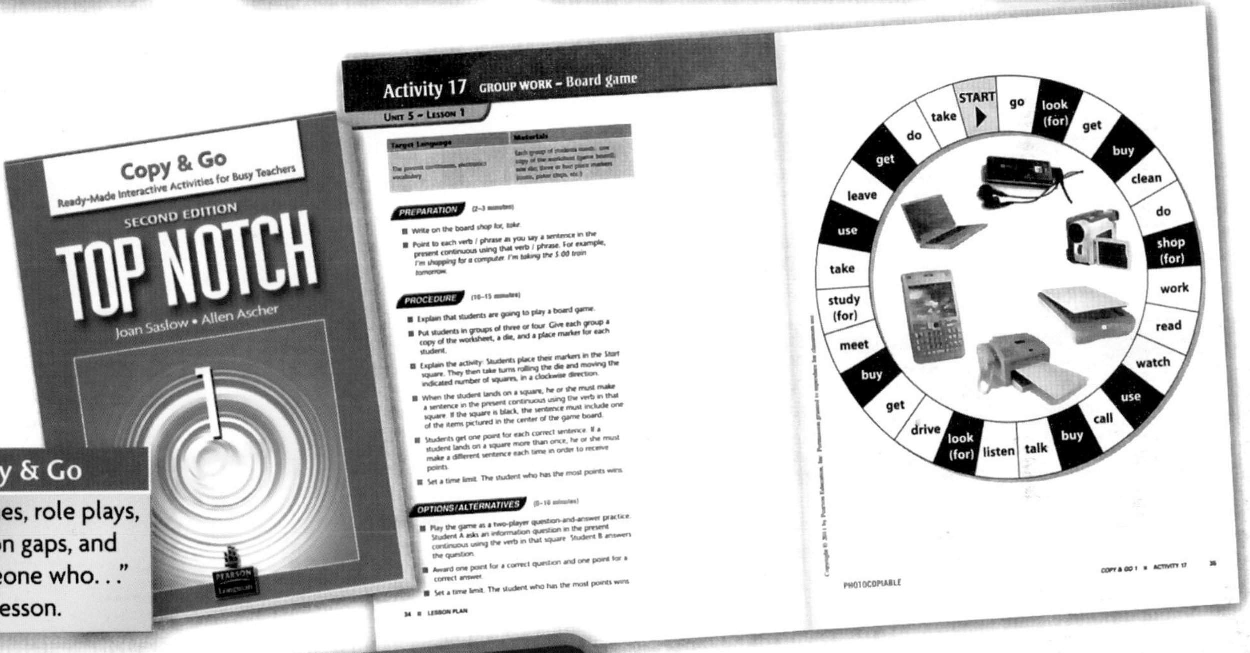

Copy & Go

Board games, role plays, information gaps, and "find someone who. . ." for every lesson.

MyTopNotchLab

An optional online learning tool with:

- An interactive *Top Notch* Workbook
- Speaking and writing activities
- Pop-up grammar help
- Student's Book *Grammar Booster* exercises
- *Top Notch TV* with extensive viewing activities
- Automatically-graded achievement tests
- Easy course management and record-keeping

UNIT 1

Getting Acquainted

Preview

GOALS After Unit 1, you will be able to:

1. Meet someone new.
2. Identify and describe people.
3. Provide personal information.
4. Introduce someone to a group.

Why are you studying English?

☐ to do business

☐ to study

☐ to travel

Did You Know?
In 2016, there will be 2 billion English speakers around the world. -from ***English Next*** (British Council)

☐ to get to know people who don't speak my language

☐ other:

Please complete the form.

Title: ☐ Mr. ☐ Mrs. ☐ Ms. ☐ Miss

Last/Family Name

First/Given Name

Nationality

Occupation

A Pair work Why are you studying English? Compare reasons with a partner.

B Class survey How many students in your class are studying English . . .

.... to do business?	.... to study?	.... (other reasons)
.... to get to know people?	.... to travel?	

C 1:02 **Photo story** Read and listen to people getting to know each other.

Susan: I'll bet this is your dad.

Cara: Yes, it is. Dad, I'd like to introduce you to my friend, Susan Grant.

Sam: It's a pleasure to meet you, Susan. Samuel Pike.

Susan: Great to meet you, too. But please, everyone calls me by my nickname, Suzy.

Sam: And just call me Sam. So, what do you do, Suzy?

Susan: I'm a photographer . . . Oh, I'm sorry. There's my husband . . . Ted, over here!

Ted: Sorry I'm late.

Susan: Ted, this is Cara's dad.

Ted: Oh, how nice to meet you, Mr. Pike!

Sam: Likewise. But please call me Sam.

> 1:03 **Formal titles**
>
> | Men | Women |
> |---|---|
> | **Mr.** | **Ms.** (married or single) |
> | | **Mrs.** (married) |
> | | **Miss** (single) |
>
> Use titles with family names, not given names.
>
> Ms. Grant NOT ~~Ms. Suzy~~

D Focus on language Look at the underlined expressions in the Photo Story. With a partner, find:

1. two expressions you can use when you introduce people.
2. three expressions you can use when you meet someone.
3. three expressions you can use when you don't want to be formal.

E Complete your response to each person.

Nice to meet you.

GIVEN NAME ______

FAMILY NAME ______

OCCUPATION ______

1 Nice to meet you, too, ...

- **a** Mr. Jerry
- **b** Mr. Rivera
- **c** Ms. Rivera

2 Good to meet you, too, ...

- **a** Ms. Watts
- **b** Ms. Naomi
- **c** Mr. Watts

F Role play Imagine your partner is a famous person. Introduce your partner to the class. Use formal titles.

> "I'd like you to meet Jerry Rivera. Mr. Rivera is a singer."

LESSON 1

GOAL Meet someone new

CONVERSATION MODEL

1:04

A Read and listen to people meeting someone new.

A: Who's that?

B: Over there? I think she's new.

A: Well, let's say hello.

. . .

B: Good morning. I'm Alex, and this is Lauren.

C: Hi. My name's Kathryn Gao. But everyone calls me Kate.

A: Great to meet you, Kate. Where are you from?

C: New York.

1:05

B **Rhythm and intonation** Listen again and repeat. Then practice the Conversation Model with two partners.

GRAMMAR *Information questions with be: Review*

Who's your teacher?	She's Ms. Nieto.
Who are they?	They're my classmates.
Where's she from?	She's from Argentina.
What city are you from?	We're from Los Angeles.
What's his e-mail address?	It's ted@kr.com [say "ted at k-r-dot-com"]
What are their names?	Andrea and Steven.
How old is your brother?	He's twenty-six.
How old are they?	She's twelve, and her little sister is eight.

Contractions

Who's = Who is	**I'm** = I am	**you're** = you are
Where's = Where is	**he's** = he is	**we're** = we are
What's = What is	**she's** = she is	**they're** = they are
	it's = it is	

GRAMMAR BOOSTER ▸ p. 123

- *Information questions with be: usage and form*
- *Possessive nouns and adjectives (review)*

A **Grammar practice** Complete the conversations. Use contractions of the verb be when possible.

1 A: .... that over there?

B: Oh, that's Hasna. .... from Lebanon.

A: .... she? She looks very young.

B: I think .... twenty-five.

2 A: Your new neighbor seems nice. .... his name?

B: His .... Ricardo.

A: .... he from?

B: Guatemala.

3 A: .... they?
B: I think .... new students.
A: .... their names?
B: Mieko and Rika.

4 A: It was nice to meet your brothers. .... they?
B: Greg's only fourteen. But my older brother, David, is twenty-eight.
A: .... David's occupation?
B: .... a lawyer.

5 A: I'll call you sometime. .... your phone number?
B: .... 555-0296. .... yours?
A: 555-8747.

6 A: .... your e-mail address? I'll send you a note.
B: .... choi23@kr.com.
A: K - r - dot - com? That's interesting. .... you from?
B: Pusan, Korea. I'm here on business.

B Grammar practice Write at least four information questions for your partner.

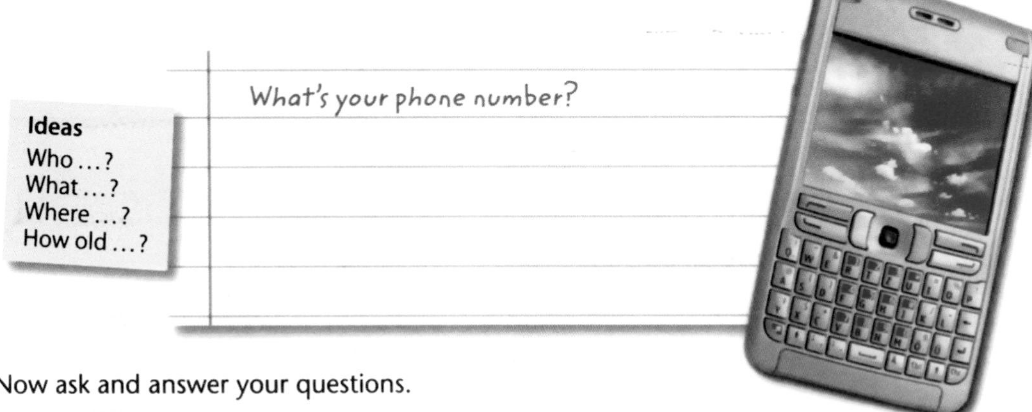

C Pair work Now ask and answer your questions.

NOW YOU CAN Meet someone new

A Role play With two partners, personalize the Conversation Model. One of you is new to your class, office, or neighborhood. Meet that person. Then change roles.

A: Who .... ?
B: Over there? I think .... new.
A: Well, let's say hello.
. . .
B: .... I'm .... and this is ....
C: .... My name's ....
A: .... Where are you from?
C: ....

Be sure to recycle this language.

Introduce people	Greet people	Shift to informality
This is ___ .	Great to meet you.	Everyone calls me ___ .
I'd like you to meet ___ .	It's a pleasure to meet you.	Just call me ___ .
I'd like to introduce you to ___ .	How nice to meet you!	Please call me ___ .

B Change partners Practice the conversation again. Meet other people.

LESSON 2

GOAL Identify and describe people

GRAMMAR Modification with adjectives: Review

Adjectives describe nouns and pronouns. They can go after the verb be or before a noun.

Alejandro Sanz is **handsome**. He's a **handsome singer** from Spain.
Tony Leung and Gong Li are **famous**. They're **famous actors** from China.

Use an article before an adjective that modifies a singular noun.

He's **a** great musician. NOT ~~He's great musician~~.

Positive adjectives
beautiful
great
excellent
famous
handsome
wonderful
fantastic
terrific

A Grammar practice On a separate sheet of paper, combine each pair of sentences.

Amy Tan is a writer. She's wonderful.
She's a wonderful writer.

1 Juan Luis Guerra is a singer. He's fantastic.
2 Penélope Cruz is an actress. She's beautiful.
3 Zhong Biao is an artist. He's excellent.
4 Alice Waters is a chef. She's famous.
5 Eric Clapton and Jeff Beck are musicians. They're great.

B Now write three sentences about other famous people.

CONVERSATION MODEL

1:06

A Read and listen to someone identify and describe a person.

A: Hey. Who's John Mayer?
B: You don't know? For real?
A: No. Is he famous?
B: He sure is. He's a great musician.
A: Where's he from?
B: The United States.

1:07

B Rhythm and intonation Listen again and repeat. Then practice the Conversation Model with a partner.

GRAMMAR Yes / no questions and short answers with be: Review

Are you our teacher?	Yes, I **am**.	No, **I'm not**.
Is she Chinese?	Yes, she **is**.	No, she **isn't**. [No, she**'s not**.]
Is your nickname Josh?	Yes, it **is**.	No, it **isn't**. [No, it**'s not**.]
Are you and Tom students?	Yes, we **are**.	No, we **aren't**. [No, we**'re not**.]
Are they famous?	Yes, they **are**.	No, they **aren't**. [No, they**'re not**.]

Be careful!
Yes, I am. NOT ~~Yes, I'm.~~
Yes, she is. NOT ~~Yes, she's.~~

GRAMMAR BOOSTER ▸ p. 124

- *Yes / no questions: usage and form*
- *Common errors*

A Find the grammar Find two information questions and one yes / no question with be in the Conversation Model on page 6.

B Grammar practice Complete the questions and answers. Use contractions when possible.

1 A: .... your father a teacher?
B: Yes, ...

2 A: .... your son an athlete?
B: No, ... an artist.

3 A: .... this your new address?
B: Yes, ...

4 A: Who .... those new students? .... from Canada?
B: No, ... I think .... from the U.K.

5 A: That's a nice hat! .... new?
B: No, ...

6 A: .... you a musician?
B: Yes, ... a violinist.

PRONUNCIATION Intonation of questions

1:08

A Use rising intonation in yes / no questions. Use falling intonation in information questions. Read and listen. Then listen again and repeat.

1 Is this his e-mail address?
2 Are they from Canada?
3 What's his e-mail address?
4 Where are they from?

B Pair work Write three yes / no questions and three information questions with be. Then take turns practicing question intonation.

NOW YOU CAN Identify and describe people

A Look at the famous people. Add information about a famous person you know.

B Pair work Use the information about the people. Change the Conversation Model to practice asking for and providing information about each person. Use your own adjective. Then change roles.

A: Hey. Who's .... ?
B: You don't know? For real?
A: No. Is .... famous?
B: .... sure is.
A: Where .... from?
B: ....

C Change partners Practice the conversation again. Talk about other famous people.

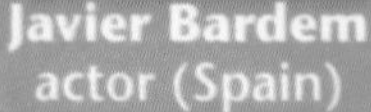

Javier Bardem
actor (Spain)

Diana Krall
musician (Canada)

Patricia Yeo
chef (U.S.)

Your own famous person

first name ....
last name ....
occupation ....
country ....
adjective to describe the person
....

GOAL Provide personal information

BEFORE YOU LISTEN

A 1:09 **Vocabulary • *Personal information*** Read and listen. Then listen again and repeat.

nationality He is originally from India, but his nationality is Canadian. He has a Canadian passport.

birthplace I'm from Mexico City, but it isn't my birthplace. I was born in a beautiful small town called Patzcuaro.

hometown She was born in Seoul, but her hometown is Pusan. She grew up there.

1:10 **Countries and nationalities**

Country	Nationality
I'm from **Japan**.	I'm **Japanese**.
She's from **China**.	She's **Chinese**.
She's from **Canada**.	She's **Canadian**.
They're from **Argentina**.	They're **Argentinean**.
He's from the **U.K.**	He's **British**.
We're from **Turkey**.	We're **Turkish**.

See page 122 for a more complete list.

B Pair work Ask your partner questions, using the Vocabulary.

"What's your birthplace?"

LISTENING COMPREHENSION

A 1:11 **Listen for details** Listen to each conversation and write each person's nationality and occupation. Then check yes or no to indicate whether the person has a nickname.

	Nationality	Occupation	Nickname?
1			☐ yes ☐ no
2			☐ yes ☐ no
3			☐ yes ☐ no
4			☐ yes ☐ no

a computer programmer

an interpreter

a graphic designer

a salesperson

B 1:12 **Infer information** Now listen to each conversation again and complete each statement.

1 He grew up in ....
  a Ankara b London c Izmir

2 Her birthplace is ....
  a Osaka b Tokyo c Seoul

3 She's originally from ....
  a Buenos Aires b Montevideo c Santiago

4 His hometown is ....
  a Chicago b Toronto c New York

NOW YOU CAN Provide personal information

Partner A: Look at the top of the page.
Partner B: Turn your book and look at the bottom of the page.
Ask information questions with be and write the missing personal information.

PARTNER A

If you don't understand, ask:
Could you repeat that?
How do you spell that?

Name: Richard Anderson
Nickname: Rick
Occupation: Photographer
Nationality: British
Birthplace: Liverpool
Age: 24
E-mail: randy@umail.com.uk

Name: Lucia Alberti
Occupation: writer
Age: 26
Nationality: Italian
Hometown: Rome
E-mail: alberti.lucia@inet.com.it

Name: Riko
Occupation: manager
Age: 42
Nationality: Japanese
Hometown: Kyoto
E-mail: ro.hira@unet.com

Name: Francisco
Nickname: Paco
Occupation: graphic designer
Nationality: Venezaelan
Age: 31
Hometown: Maracaibo
E-mail: fp52@vmail.com.ve

PARTNER B

If you don't understand, ask:
Could you repeat that?
How do you spell that?

Name: Richard
Nickname: Rick
Occupation: photographer
Nationality: British
Birthplace: Liverpool
Age: 24
E-mail: ....

Name: Lucian
Occupation: writer
Age: 26
Nationality: Italian
Hometown: Rome
E-mail: ....

Name: Riko Ohira
Occupation: manager
Age: 42
Nationality: Japanese
Hometown: Kyoto
E-mail: rohira@unet.com.jp

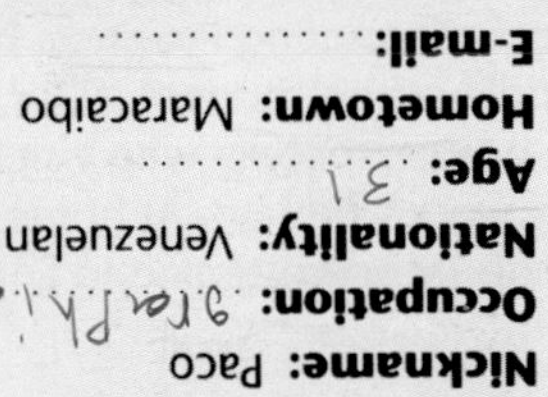

Name: Francisco Pastor
Nickname: Paco
Occupation: graphic
Nationality: Venezuelan
Age: 31
Hometown: Maracaibo
E-mail: ....

LESSON 3

GOAL Introduce someone to a group

BEFORE YOU READ

A Warm-up In your life, where do you see or hear English?

B Preview Before you read, search for the word English in the article. Then answer this question: How does each person use English?

READING

1:13 

Who Uses English?

MEET LETICIA MARQUES. She works as a financial manager for a Swedish automotive company in Curitiba, Brazil, where she was born and raised. She is single and lives with her parents. "I use English every day," Ms. Marques says. "We use it in most of our e-mails and meetings and for calls to Sweden, the U.S., and France." In her free time, she likes to watch DVDs in English. "It's good for my pronunciation," she says.

THIS IS YUAN YONG JING, his wife, Zheng Yang, and their son, Yuan Bao. They live in Beijing, China. Mr. Yuan, a manager, is originally from Weihai, a small seaside city in Shandong Province. His wife is a teacher, and their son is a middle-school student. "Our company provides tour guides to foreign businesspeople who visit China, so English is very important for my work," he says. At home, Mr. Yuan enjoys watching English-language TV and listening to English-language radio.

MEET MARCUS STOLZE, an information technology researcher. Mr. Stolze lives with his wife, Thérèse, and children, Lena and Jan, in Rüti, a small town in Switzerland. Mr. Stolze is originally from Brilon, Germany. Thérèse is an English teacher and speaks four languages. Their children are also multilingual. "At work, we use English a lot because we communicate with people who speak many different languages," he says. "Also, most good books on computing are in English," he adds.

Source: Authentic interviews of real people

A Infer information Complete each statement.

1 ...... are in English at Ms. Marques's company in Brazil.
  a E-mails
  b Meetings
  c Phone calls
  d E-mails, meetings, and calls

2 In his work, Mr. Yuan uses English ....
  a to teach classes
  b to help businesspeople
  c to watch TV
  d to listen to the radio

3 Mr. Stolze probably uses English with people from ....
  a the United States
  b Switzerland
  c the United Kingdom
  d all over the world

B Scan for facts Complete the information about the people.

	Ms. Marques	Mr. Yuan	Mr. Stolze
Occupation			
Lives in . . .			
Hometown			
Married?	☐ yes ☐ no	☐ yes ☐ no	☐ yes ☐ no

On your *ActiveBook* Self-Study Disc:
Extra Reading Comprehension Questions

NOW YOU CAN Introduce someone to a group

A Read the information about each person. Then complete the two paragraphs below.

Name: Evelyne Hsu
Nickname: Effie
Occupation: office assistant
Hometown: Chia-yi, Taiwan
Birthplace: same
Age: 27
Favorite actor: Tony Leung
Favorite sport: swimming
Other: lives in Kaohsiung

This is ...., but everyone calls her .... She's .... years old and she's an .... Ms. .... lives in .... but she is originally from a city called .... Her favorite actor is ...., and her favorite sport is ....

Name: José Antonio Méndez
Nickname: Tonio
Occupation: market researcher
Hometown: Celanova, a small town in Spain
Birthplace: Equatorial Guinea (in Africa)
Age: 48
Other: lives in New York, has two children

Meet .... He's a ...., and he lives in .... Everyone calls him .... He's originally from ...., but actually he was born in .... Mr. Méndez is .... years old, and he has ....

B Notepadding Interview a classmate. Write his or her personal information on the notepad.

Name:
Nickname:
Occupation:
Hometown:
Birthplace:
Age:
Favorite actor:
Favorite sport:
Other:

C Group work Introduce your partner to your classmates.

Be sure to recycle this language.

This is ___.
I'd like you to meet ___.
I'd like to introduce you to ___.
Everyone calls her / him ___.
His / her nickname is ___.
___ is originally from ___.
His / her hometown is ___.
His / her favorite ___ is ___.

Review

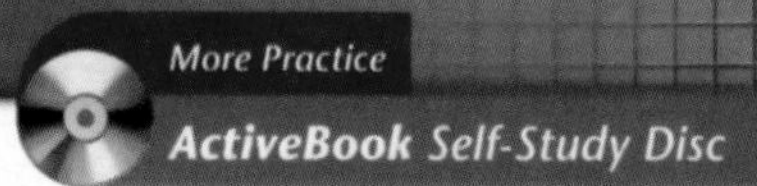

grammar · vocabulary · listening
reading · speaking · pronunciation

1:14

A **Listening comprehension** Listen to the conversations. Then listen again and write each person's occupation and nationality.

	Name	Occupation	Nationality
1	George Detcheverry		
2	Sonia Pereira		
3	Mark Zaleski		
4	Marjorie Baxter		

Polish
French
Brazilian
Australian

B Complete each statement.

1 We're from (China / Chinese).
2 He's (Australia / Australian).
3 She's from (Italy / Italian).
4 My friend is (Uruguay / Uruguayan).
5 We're from (Japan / Japanese).
6 They're (Chile / Chilean).
7 My neighbors are from (Korea / Korean).
8 We're (Mexico / Mexican).

C Complete each conversation in your own way. (You don't need to give real information.)

1 "What city are you from?"
YOU ....
2 "What's your e-mail address?"
YOU ....
3 "Are you a teacher?"
YOU ....
4 YOU .... ?
"I'm from Canada."
5 YOU .... ?
"I'm a graphic designer."
6 YOU ....
"Great to meet you, too."

D **Writing** On a separate sheet of paper, write a short description of the classmate you interviewed on page 11. Include the following information.

- first and last name
- age
- occupation
- hometown
- birthplace

My partner's first name is Peter. His last name is Hughes. He is twenty…

1:15/1:16
Top Notch Pop
"It's Nice to Meet You"
Lyrics p. 149

WRITING BOOSTER ▸ p. 142
- *Capitalization*
- *Guidance for Exercise D*

ORAL REVIEW

Pair work

1 Create a conversation for the people in Picture 1. Start like this:

Who's Ricky Martin?

2 With a partner, invent personal information for the people in Picture 2. Then create a conversation for them.

Contest Form teams. Create questions for another team about the web page, using the verb be. (A team gets one point for each correct question and one point for each correct answer.) For example:

What's his nickname?

UNIT 2

Going Out

Preview

GOALS After Unit 2, you will be able to:

1. Accept or decline an invitation.
2. Express locations and give directions.
3. Make plans to see an event.
4. Talk about musical tastes.

My Tunes STORE

GENRES
- Rhythm & Blues
- Reggae
- Rock
- Salsa
- Classical Music
- Folk Music
- Movie Soundtracks
- Jazz
- Show Tunes

FREE DOWNLOADS
- Albums
- Singles

FEATURES
- Add to Facebook
- Buy MP3s

QUICK LINKS
- Browse
- Search
- Redeem
- Support
- My Alerts
- My Account

THIS WEEK'S SPECIALS

See All

Rhythm & Blues

Reggae

Rock

Salsa

Classical Music

Folk Music

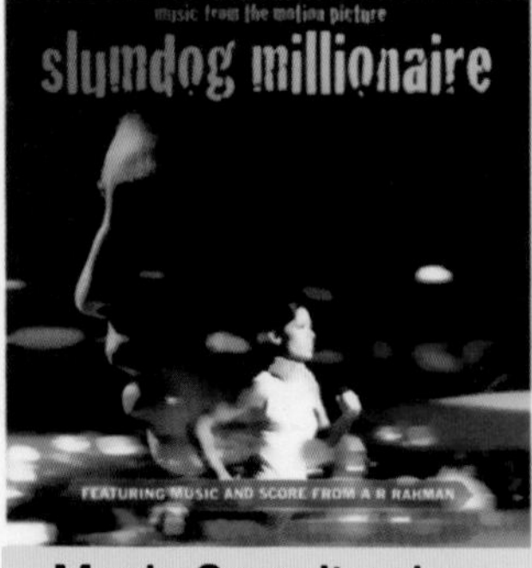

Movie Soundtracks

Jazz

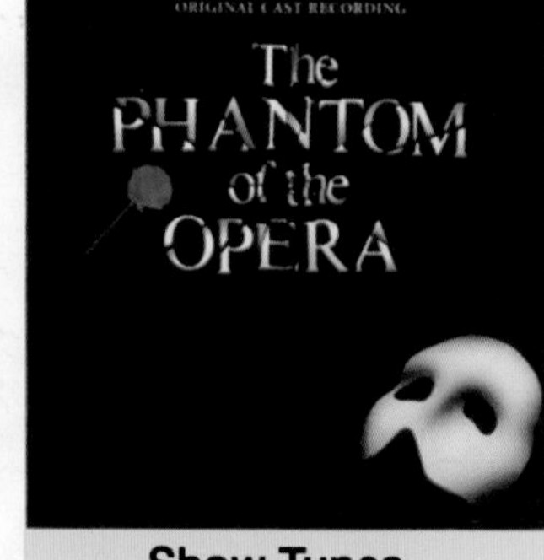

Show Tunes

A Look at the online music store site. Do you download music from the Internet? Why or why not?

B 1:17 **Vocabulary • *Genres*** Listen and repeat.

C **Pair work** Tell your partner what you would click on first. Explain why.

D **Discussion** Which is better—buying a CD in a store or downloading music from the Internet? Explain your answer.

1:18

E Photo story Read and listen to a conversation about music.

Meg: Hey. What's up?

Sara: Not much. Just downloading some new songs.

Meg: Downloading? That's not for me! Too much trouble. How about some live music tonight?

Sara: Sounds good. Where?

Meg: Klepto's playing at midnight at the Spot. Would you like to go?

Sara: At midnight? Sorry. That's past my bedtime.

Meg: Well, River T's there, too. They're playing at 8:00.

Sara: River T—the R&B group? Now that's more my style. I'm a real R&B fan.

Meg: Perfect! Meet you in front of the club at 7:45?

Sara: See you there!

F Focus on language Choose the underlined word or expression from the Photo Story with the same meaning:

1 That's too late for me.
2 Great!
3 music in a concert
4 What are you doing?
5 I like that better.
6 I don't like that.

G Think and explain Choose an answer. Use a quotation to explain your answer.

1 What's Sara doing?
  a getting music from the Internet
  b buying tickets for a concert on the Internet

"Sara says, 'Just downloading some new songs.'"

2 What does Meg want to do?
  a download music from the Internet
  b go to a concert

3 Which woman doesn't like to go to sleep late?
  a Sara
  b Meg

4 When and where are they going to meet?
  a at midnight at River T
  b at the club before the show

H What kinds of music do you like? Number the music genres in order, making number 1 your favorite.

.... salsa
.... movie soundtracks
.... pop
.... rock
.... classical
.... reggae
.... hip-hop
.... jazz
.... other ....

I Class survey Compare your choices. Which genres do most classmates like?

"Who chose rock as their favorite?"

an electric guitar

LESSON 1

GOAL Accept or decline an invitation

CONVERSATION MODEL

A 1:19 Read and listen to an invitation to a movie.

A: Are you free on Saturday? *Batman* is at the Movie Center.

B: Really? I'd love to go. What time?

A: At noon.

To decline . . .

B: Really? I'd love to go, but I'm busy on Saturday.

A: Too bad. Maybe some other time.

B 1:20 **Rhythm and intonation** Listen again and repeat. Then practice the Conversation Model with a partner.

GRAMMAR Prepositions of time and place; Questions with When, What time, and Where: Review

Prepositions of time

When's the concert? **What time's** the play? It's . . .

on	in	at
on Saturday	in March	at 8:30
on June 7th	in 2009	at noon
on Monday, May 3rd	in the summer	at midnight
on Tuesday morning	in the morning	
	in ten minutes	

Prepositions of place

Where's the play? It's . . .

on	in	at
on Fifth Avenue	in Mexico	at the Film Forum
on the corner	in Osaka	at work
on the street	in the park	at school
on the left	in the neighborhood	at the art gallery

Contractions
When's = When is
What time's = What time is
Where's = Where is

GRAMMAR BOOSTER ▸ p. 125
- *Prepositions of time and place: usage*

Grammar practice Complete the e-mail message with prepositions of time and place.

From: jjlove@meltdown.net
To: bonnie@vmail.com
Subject: Salsa dance concert

Hi, Bonnie: Are you busy ___on___ Tuesday evening? There's a salsa dance concert right near your office ___at___ the Mellon Exhibit Space. Sounds like something really special with dancers from all over the world. It starts ___at___ 8:30. I'll be ___at___ work until 6:00, but I could meet you ___at___ 6:15 or 6:30 ___on___ the corner of Grand and Crane. We could have something to eat before the concert. What do you think? —JJ

VOCABULARY *Entertainment and cultural events*

1:21

A Read and listen. Then listen again and repeat.

a movie / a film

a play

a concert

a talk / a lecture

an art exhibit

B Pair work Ask and answer questions about the events in the pictures above. Use When, Where, and What time.

"Where's the talk?"

"It's at Book World."

1:22

C Listening comprehension Listen to the conversations and complete the chart.

	Kind of event	Time of event	Does the person want to go? (Write yes, no, or maybe.)
1		sunday	✓
2	movie		✓
3	play		✓
4	concert	7:45	

1:23

D Listen to the conversations again. Match the event and the place.

...b... **1** *Agamemnon*
...a... **2** the Boston Symphony Orchestra
...c... **3** *Bus Stop*
...d... **4** Nick Hornby

a at the Cinema Center
b at the City Nights Bookstore
c at the Theater in the Circle
d at the Festival

NOW YOU CAN Accept or decline an invitation

A Pair work Change the Conversation Model. Use these events or other events. Decide to accept or decline. Then change roles.

A: Are you free ....? .... is at ....

B: Really? ....

Don't stop!
If you decline, suggest a different event.

Be sure to recycle this language.

That's past my bedtime.
That's not for me.
That's more my style.

B Change partners Practice the conversation again. Use different events.

LESSON 2

GOAL Express locations and give directions

CONVERSATION MODEL

A 1:24 Read and listen to someone asking for and getting directions.

A: Excuse me. I'm looking for the National Bank.

B: The National Bank? Do you know the address?

A: Yes. It's 205 Holly Avenue.

B: Oh. Walk to the corner of First and Holly. It's right around the corner, across from the museum.

Or if you don't know . . .

B: The National Bank? I'm sorry. I'm not from around here.

A: Thanks, anyway.

B 1:25 **Rhythm and intonation** Listen again and repeat. Then practice the Conversation Model with a partner.

VOCABULARY *Locations and directions*

A 1:26 Read and listen. Then listen again and repeat.

Locations Where is the ____?

It's **on the right side** of the street.

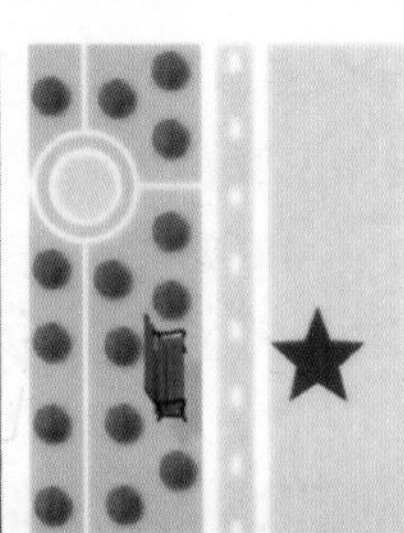

It's **across from** the park.

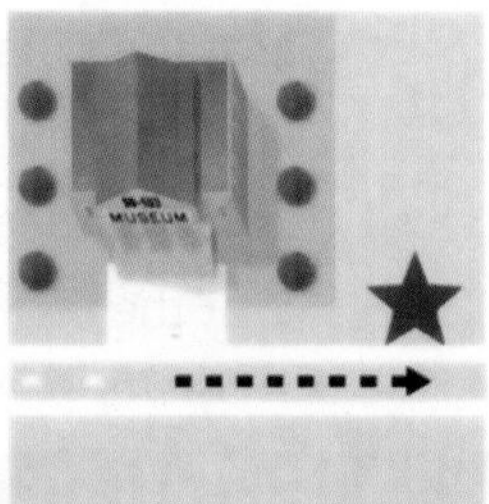

It's **down the street from** the museum.

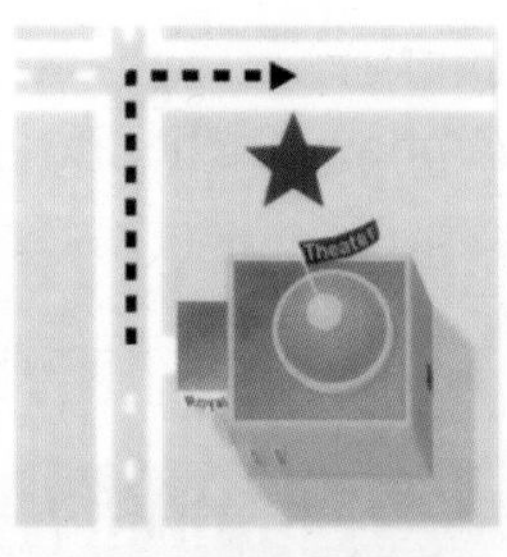

It's **around the corner from** the theater.

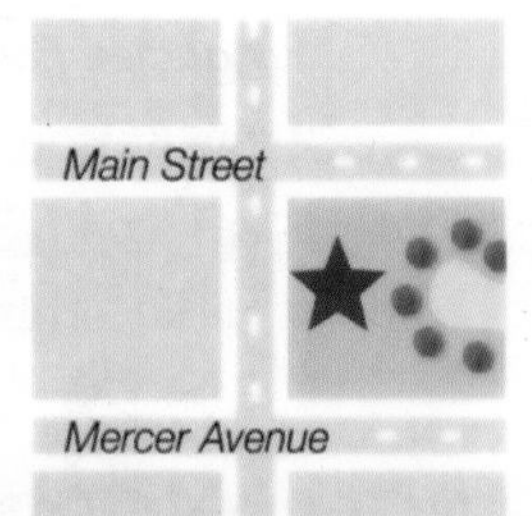

It's **between** Main (Street) **and** Mercer (Avenue).

Directions How do I get to the ____?

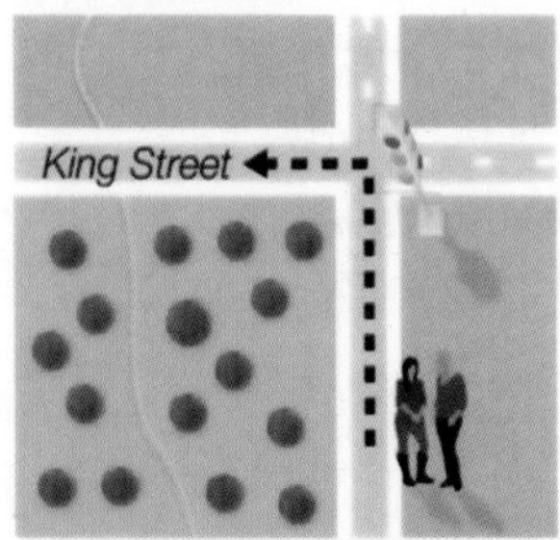

Turn left at the corner / **at** the light / **on** King Street.

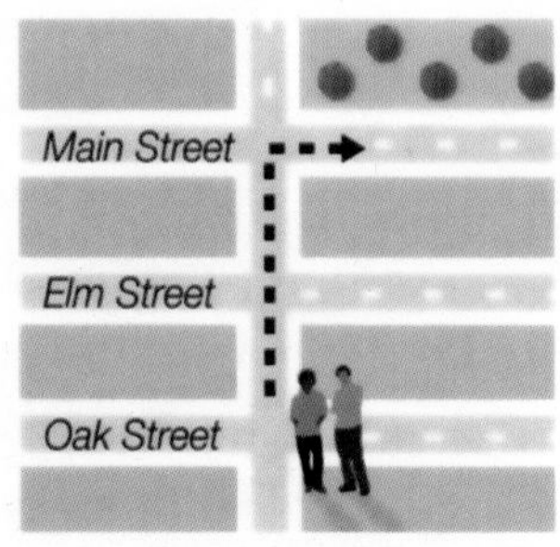

Go / Walk / Drive **two blocks and turn right.**

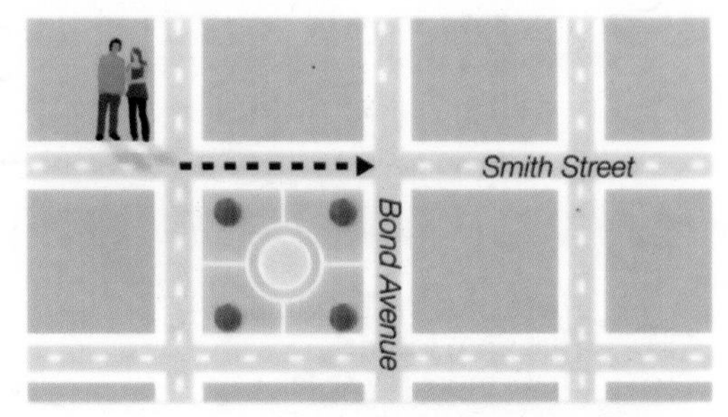

Go / Walk / Drive **to the corner of** Smith (Street) **and** Bond (Avenue).

B 1:27 **Listening comprehension** Listen to the conversations and write the number of each place the people talk about on the map. (Be careful: There are three places but seven boxes.)

OCEAN CITY
HUDSON STREET
ADRIATIC
INDIAN
PACIFIC
ATLANTIC STREET
STREET
STREET
STREET
BALTIC STREET
STREET
BAY STREET

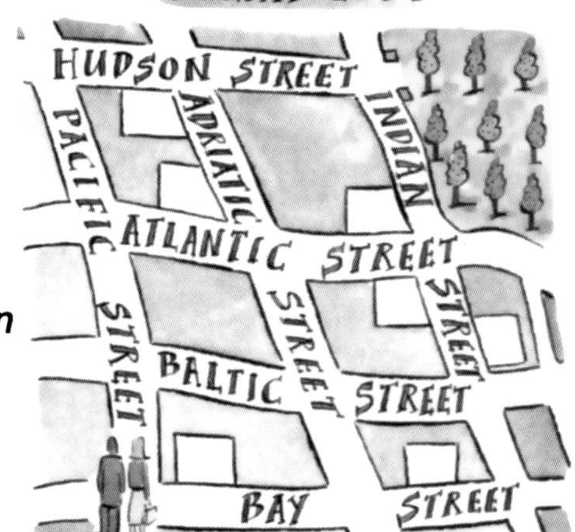

C Pair work Use the vocabulary of location to tell your partner where you live.

> "My house is on Grove Street, between Dodd Street and Park Street."

PRONUNCIATION *Rising intonation to confirm information*

A 1:28 Repeat information with rising intonation to be sure you understand. Read and listen. Then listen again and repeat.

A: Where's the library?
B: The library?

A: Let's meet at the mall.
B: The mall?

B Pair work Talk about two other places to practice confirming information.

NOW YOU CAN Express locations and give directions

A Pair work Use the Vocabulary and the Piermont map (or a map of your own town or neighborhood) to change the Conversation Model. Then change roles.

A: Excuse me. I'm looking for ....
B: ....? Do you know the address?
A: Yes. It's ....
B: Oh. ....

Don't stop!
Ask about other locations.

THE PIERMONT MUSEUM OF ART
204
HOLLY AVENUE
BOOK WORLD
85
SECOND AVENUE
CLARK STREET
THE DANCE PALACE
83
DANCE PALACE
THE NATIONAL BANK
205
FILM FORUM
127
THE FILM FORUM
128
FIRST STREET
MOONBUCKS COFFEE 1
126
THE TAFT SYMPHONY HALL
MOONBUCKS COFFEE 2
121
HARPER AVENUE
101
THE BELL THEATER
YOU ARE HERE.
PIERMONT
Entertainment
District

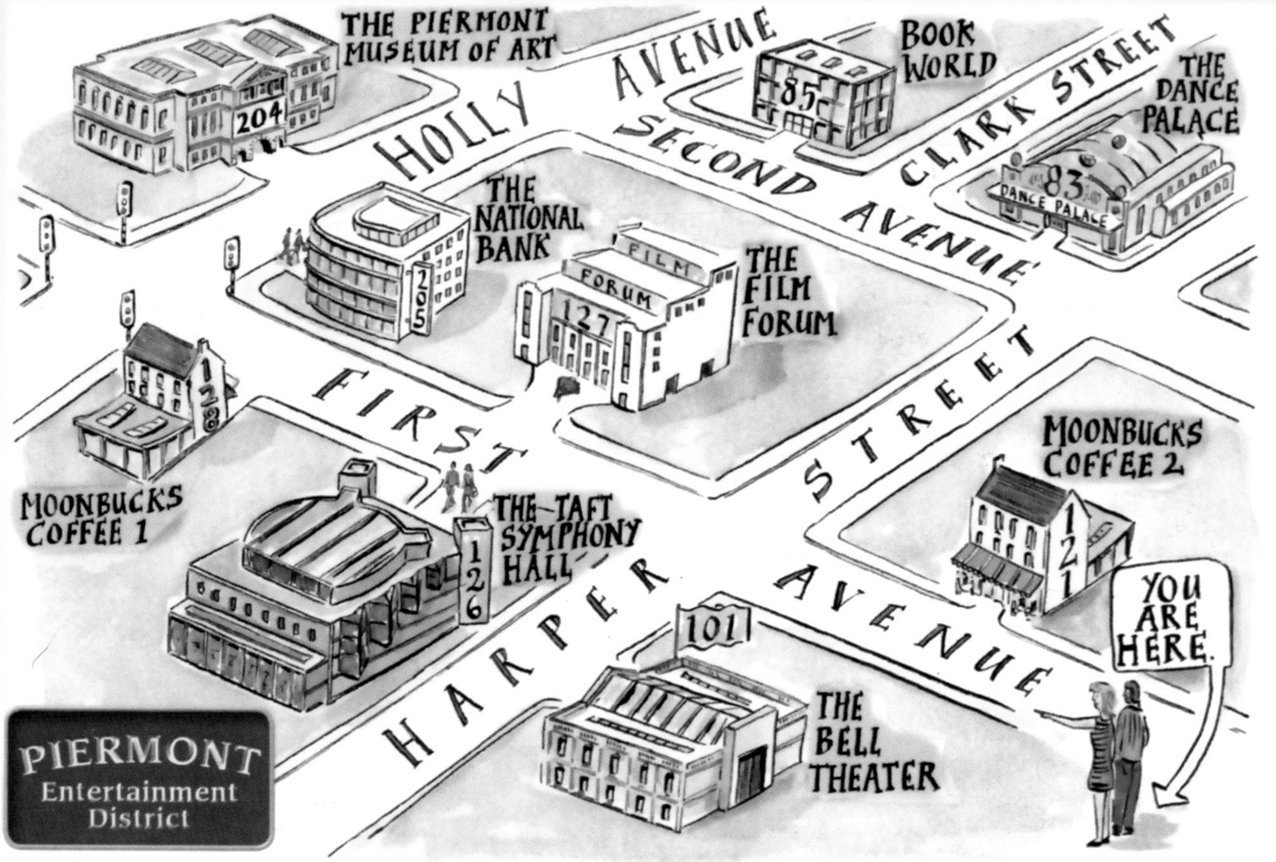

B Change partners Ask about other locations and give directions.

LESSON 3

GOAL Make plans to see an event

BEFORE YOU LISTEN

Preview Look at the tickets below. What kinds of events are included in the Kingston Culturefest?

LISTENING COMPREHENSION

1:29

A Listen for details Listen to people calling the Kingston Culturefest. Look at the tickets. Then listen again and complete the information in the boxes.

1

Culture fest KINGSTON

Classic Film Series

Date: May ____ **Time:** 7:00 P.M.

Location: Lamont Theater 75 66th Street

Price: $ 10

Event: *Nice to Meet You* and *The 39 Steps*

2

Culture fest KINGSTON

Date: May ____ **Time:** 2:00 P.M.

Location: Natural History Museum at 110 Greenway

Price: free

Event: History of Latin Music Lecture/Concert

Seat: ____

Seat: ____

3

Culture fest KINGSTON

Date: May ____ **Time:** 7:30 P.M.

Location: Kingston Concert Hall 3600 Central Avenue

Event: Ludacris Hip-Hop Series

Price: $ 25 **Seat:** ____

Price: $ ____ **Seat:** ____

4

Culture fest KINGSTON

Date: May ____ **Time:** 11:00 P.M.

Location: Kingston Gallery ____ 260 Central Avenue

Price: $ 50

Event: *The Lion King* **Seat:** 10a

Event: *The Lion King* **Seat:** 10b

5

Culture fest KINGSTON

Date: May 9 **Time:** ____ P.M.

Location: Kingston Gallery ____ at 109 Greenway

Price: $ ____

Event: Picasso: His Life and Art

Seat: 7G

1:30

B Listen for locations Look at the map of the entertainment district of Kingston. Listen again and write the number of each place in its location on the map. (Be careful: There are five places but ten boxes.)

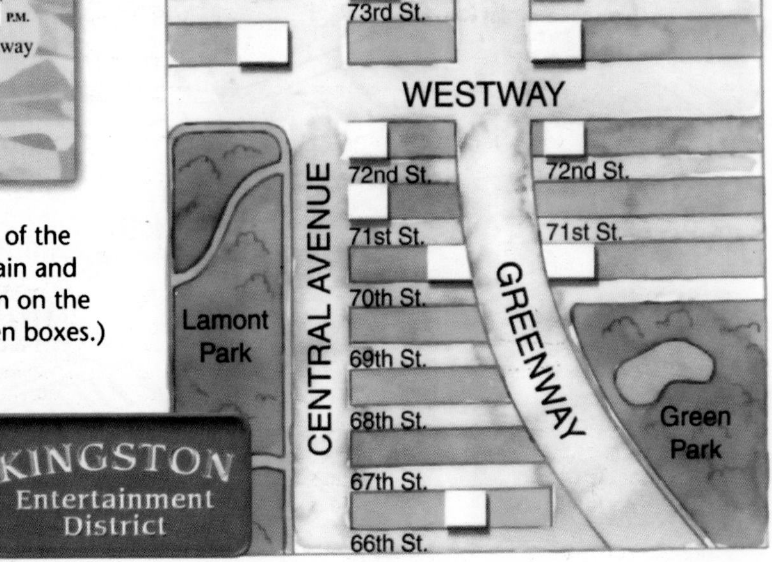

NOW YOU CAN Make plans to see an event

A Notepadding Read about all the events for the week of May 6–12 below and on the tickets on page 20. Choose events you'd like to see. Write those events, times, and places on the notepad.

Event	Day / Date / Time	Place

Kingston Post

THIS WEEK at the KINGSTON Culture fest HIGHLIGHTS

MAY						
MON	TUES	WED	THURS	FRI	SAT	SUN
6	7	8	9	10	11	12

THEATER

Neil Simon's classic comedy
Barefoot in the Park
Lamont Theater

Tuesday to Friday 8:00 P.M.
Tkts: Balcony from $65
Orchestra from $85

The Indian Ink Theatre Company
The Dentist's Chair

"A Serious Play For Serious Theatergoers"

Kingston Gallery 2
Friday and Saturday 8:00 P.M.

TALKS / LECTURES

Global Warming: How It Changes Our World

Al Gore (former vice president of the U.S. and winner of the Nobel Prize)
Tuesday 6:30 P.M. and 9:00 P.M.
Natural History Museum
Free!

GALLERY TALK
The History of Art
Series of Six Lectures
This week: Greek and Roman art with art exhibit included.
Janetta Rebold Benton

Monday and Thursday 7:45 P.M.
Kingston Gallery 2
Members' price: $5.00
General admission: $12.00

CONCERTS

Vanessa-Mae, **violinist**
Vanessa-Mae will play the Tchaikovsky Violin Concerto in D Major with the New York Philharmonic Orchestra
Also: Johann Sebastian Bach's *Toccata and Fugue in D Minor*
Kingston Concert Hall
Wednesday and Saturday: 8:00 P.M.
Sunday: 2:00 P.M. (matinee)
Tkts: $50 (students $25)

GALLERY JAZZ
Cassandra
Wilson

Singer, songwriter, producer sings from her new album *Loverly*, featuring "Dust my Broom."
Kingston Gallery 2
Tuesday, Wednesday, and Friday 10:00 P.M.
late show: **12:30 A.M.** Tkts: $23

B Pair work Compare the events you'd like to see. Make plans to see one or more of the events together. Use the map on page 20.

Be sure to recycle this language.

Invite
Are you free / busy on ___?
There's a [play] at ___.
Would you like to go?

Ask for information
How about ___?
What time's the ___?
Where is it?

Accept and decline
I'd love to go.
See you at ___.
I'd love to go, but ___.
Maybe some other time.
That's past my bedtime.
I'm [not really] a ___ fan.
That's not for me.
That's more my style.

Locations / Directions
It's across from the ___.
It's around the corner from the ___.
It's on the ___ side of the street.
It's between ___ and ___.
Turn left at ___.
Go (Walk / Drive) to ___.

LESSON 4

GOAL Talk about musical tastes

BEFORE YOU READ

A Warm-up In what ways is music important to you?

B Preview Read the question at the beginning of the article and the first sentence in each answer. What do you think "musical tastes" are?

READING

1:31

What are your musical tastes?

My favorite genre is alternative rock. I love live concerts. I once saw Metallica and Foo Fighters live in New York. They were awesome. I also like to listen to music when I travel. I just load my mini MP3 player with lots of songs and carry it with me. At home, I like the music channels on TV. I also enjoy music videos and often search for them on the Internet.

Damir Rudic
Systems administrator, IT, Banja Luka City, Bosnia and Herzegovina

I'm a big music fan. I'm into all kinds of music—pop, R&B, jazz, classical—you name it. When I'm really stressed out, classical music helps me relax. I also like to play "oldies" and sing along really loud! In the past, I collected CDs, but now I just buy songs on the Internet. It's really convenient because you don't have to change CDs! I just download the files onto my MP3 player.

Moon-Jeong Curie Lim
Marketing manager, Seoul, Korea

I listen to music on my commute and at home after work. I've got plenty of time to listen because I listen while I do other things, like reading, checking e-mail, or hanging out with friends. I love to see rock bands live, but sometimes I prefer CDs because the sound quality is better. I download music and I pay about one U.S. dollar per song, but even at that price I could never buy all the music I want to listen to!

Adam Klagsbrun
Sales representative, New York, USA

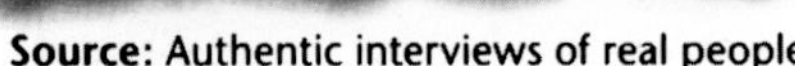

Source: Authentic interviews of real people

A Identify supporting details Read the interviews again. Circle T for <u>true</u> or F for <u>false</u> about each statement. Find details in the text to support your answers.

(T) F	**1**	Mr. Rudic likes music videos. He says:	T
T (F)	**2**	Mr. Rudic only listens to music at home. He says:	
T (F)	**3**	Ms. Lim buys lots of CDs in stores. She says:	
T (F)	**4**	Mr. Klagsbrun always prefers live concerts to CDs. He says:	

B Make personal comparisons Who are you like: Mr. Rudic, Ms. Lim, or Mr. Klagsbrun? Explain how.

"I'm like Adam Klagsbrun. I listen to music while I do other things."

NOW YOU CAN Talk about musical tastes

On your *ActiveBook* Self-Study Disc: **Extra Reading Comprehension Questions**

A Frame your ideas Fill out the survey about your musical tastes.

MUSIC IN YOUR LIFE TAKE THE SURVEY!

1. Are you a music fan?
- ☑ yes
- ○ no

2. What's your favorite kind of music?
- ○ rock ○ pop ☑ classical
- ○ jazz ○ R&B ○ rap / hip-hop
- ○ Latin ○ folk ○ other ....

3. Who are your favorite artists?

....

....

Why? ....

....

4. When do you listen to music?
- ○ when I study ☑ when I drive
- ○ when I work ○ all the time
- ○ other ....

5. Do you go to concerts?
- ○ often ○ sometimes ☑ never

If so, what's your favorite kind of concert?

....

6. How do you listen to music?
- ☑ on CDs ○ on the Internet
- ○ on the radio ○ on music videos
- ○ on MP3s ○ on TV music channels
- ○ on cassettes ○ other ....

7. How many CDs do you own?
- ☑ none ○ 1–50 ○ 50–100 ○ 100–200
- ○ more than 200

What kinds of music? classical

....

B Pair work Compare surveys with a partner. Summarize your answers and your partner's answers on the notepad.

About me	About my partner
I'm a hip-hop fan.	*Her favorite music is hip-hop, too.*

C Discussion Now use the notepad to tell the class about your musical tastes.

"My partner and I are really into music. We're both hip-hop fans."

Text-mining (optional)
Underline language in the Reading on page 22 to use in the Discussion. For example: "I'm into ____."

Review

grammar · vocabulary · listening
reading · speaking · pronunciation

A 1:32 **Listening comprehension** Listen to the conversations about entertainment and cultural events. Complete the chart with the kind of event and the time of the event.

	Kind of event	Time of event
1		
2		
3		

B 1:33 Look at the chart and listen again. Circle the event if the person accepts the invitation.

C Complete each conversation, based on the picture.

1 

A: There's a great .... at the City Theater.
B: .... 's the show?
A: Eight o'clock.

2 

A: I'm sorry I'm late. This .... is awesome. What time did it start?
B: .... 6:30. Don't worry. You didn't miss much.

3

A: Hello?
B: Hi. I'm calling from the Beekman Gallery. There's an .... of paintings from France.
A: Sounds great! Meet you there .... fifteen minutes?

4 

A: Are you free .... Monday evening? Dr. Benson is giving a .... on the native plants of the desert. Do you want to go?
B: That depends. .... time?
A: It's .... 7:00.

D Unscramble the following sentences. Then match the sentences with the pictures. Write the number on the picture.

1 on Martine The bookstore Avenue Street is corner of and the Bank

....

2 8:00 Saturday The exhibit is on August 3 at P.M.

....

3 around the street The movie is the theater corner and down

....

4 corner The house is around the street and across the

....

E Writing On a separate sheet of paper, write at least five sentences about yourself and your tastes in music.

My name is Kazu Sato. I'm from Nagoya. I'm a classical music fan. I love Mozart...

WRITING BOOSTER ▸ p. 142
- *The sentence*
- *Guidance for Exercise E*

1:34/1:35 **Top Notch Pop**
"Going Out"
Lyrics p. 149

ORAL REVIEW

Contest Form teams. Study the ads for one minute. Then close your books. With your team, name all the events you can remember. (Your team gets one point for each correct event.)

Pair work Create conversations for the two people.

1 Ask and answer questions about the ads. Use Where, When, and What time. For example:

Q: Where's the lecture?
A: It's . . .

2 Discuss the ads. Make plans, suggestions, and invitations. Discuss your likes and dislikes.

The Journal News- October 22

Today's Entertainment

B16

MOVIES

In a world where anything could happen, at any time . . .

" A hilarious spoof of airport culture"
Alizia Compton, *Today's Arts Magazine*

Do You Have Any Liquids?

Mama Cruz Rachel Weldon

CinePlex 2

5:25, 7:05, 9:30

PLAYS

MUSIC

Nora Jones
singer / songwriter
TODAY ONLY
City Limits Jazz Club
9:30 P.M.

The China Philharmonic Orchestra with The Shanghai Opera House Chorus
Mozart's Requiem
Symphony Hall, 8:00 P.M.

OTHER EVENTS - Talks/Lectures

James M Cowan
A Plan for Everyday Life
Lecture, discussion, book signing
Books and Other Precious Things
400 Jackson Street 6:45 P.M.

NOW I CAN...

- ☐ Accept or decline an invitation.
- ☐ Express locations and give directions.
- ☐ Make plans to see an event.
- ☐ Talk about musical tastes.

Preview

The Extended Family

GOALS After Unit 3, you will be able to:

1 Report news about relationships.
2 Describe extended families.
3 Compare people.
4 Discuss family cultural traditions.

I'm Linda. This is my husband, Tom. And this is my family.

grandparents

my **grandfather** — Cliff | my **grandmother** — Helen

parents

my .... — Mary | my .... — Mark

my **uncle** — Jack | my **aunt** — Sally

my **cousins** — Pete, Pam

in-laws

my **mother-in-law** — Fran | my **father-in-law** — Dan

my **sister-in-law** — Rita | my .... — Bill

my **nephew** — Evan | my **niece** — Kim

my .... — Jane

children

my .... — Kevin | my .... — Kaye

my **brother-in-law** — Paul

A Look at Linda's photo album. Fill in the missing words in the yellow boxes.

B 2:02 **Vocabulary** • ***The extended family***
Listen and repeat.

C **Pair work** Ask and answer questions about Linda's relatives. Use Who.

"Who's Bill's wife?"
"Rita."
"Who are Mary and Mark?"
"They're Tom's in-laws."

D 2:03 **Photo story** Read and listen to two women discussing family photos.

Anna: Who's that guy? Your brother?

Jane: No, that's my brother-in-law, David. He's married to my older sister, Laura. And this is their son, Michael. He's adopted.*

Anna: Do they have any other children?

Jane: Just the one. He's an only child.

Anna: Looks like they're having a great time in New York.

Jane: Actually, they live there.

Anna: They do? Wow! How often do you see them?

Jane: About twice a year.

Anna: And what about these kids?

Jane: They're my younger sister's. Vicky's the girl. And these are her little brothers, Nick and Alex.

Anna: Nick and Alex look so much alike! Are they twins?*

Jane: They are. My sister and her kids all live in Hong Kong.

*adopted: David and Laura aren't Michael's birth parents.

*twins: Nick and Alex were born at the same time.

E **Think and explain** Check true, false, or no info.
Then explain each answer, using information from the Photo Story.

	true	false	no info
1 David is the husband of Anna's older sister.	☐	☐	☐
2 David and Laura have two children.	☐	☐	☐
3 Jane is Laura's younger sister.	☐	☐	☐
4 Jane doesn't have any brothers.	☐	☐	☐
5 Jane has two nieces and one nephew.	☐	☐	☐
6 Vicky, Nick, and Alex are Jane's cousins.	☐	☐	☐

"He's Jane's brother-in-law, not Anna's."

F Complete the chart with information about your extended family.
Write the number of people in each category.

I have . . .		
___ brother(s)	___ uncle(s)	___ cousin(s)
___ sister(s)	___ aunt(s)	___ brother(s)-in-law
___ nephew(s)	___ niece(s)	___ sister(s)-in-law

G **Group work** Compare charts with your classmates.
Who in your class has a very large extended family?

"How many ___s do you have?"

LESSON 1

GOAL Report news about relationships

VOCABULARY Relationships and marital status

A 2:04 Read and listen. Then listen again and repeat.

They're **single**.

They're **engaged**.
(He's her **fiancé**. / She's his **fiancée**.)

They're **married**.

They're **separated**.

They're **divorced**.
(He's her **ex-husband**. / She's his **ex-wife**.)

She's **widowed**.

B 2:05 **Listening comprehension** Listen to the conversations. Circle the word that completes each statement.

1 The woman is (single / engaged / married).
2 His aunt is (engaged / widowed / divorced).
3 His sister is (engaged / separated / divorced).
4 Her sister is (engaged / separated / divorced).

GRAMMAR The simple present tense: Review

Affirmative statements

I **live** in Rio.
I **have** two children.
I **work** in a school.

Claire **lives** in Tokyo.
She **has** one daughter.
She **works** in an office.

Negative statements

I **don't live** in Lima.
I **don't have** any children.

Paul **doesn't live** in Seoul.
He **doesn't have** a son.

Yes / no questions and short answers

Do you **have** any cousins?
Yes, I **do**. / No, I **don't**.

Do they **work** nearby?
Yes, they **do**. / No, they **don't**.

Does she **have** any children?
Yes, she **does**. / No, she **doesn't**.

Does he **work** nearby?
Yes, he **does**. / No, he **doesn't**.

Contractions
don't = do not
doesn't = does not

GRAMMAR BOOSTER ▸ p. 126
• *The simple present tense: usage and form*

Grammar practice Complete the questions and answers. Use the simple present tense.

1 (have) A: Does your cousin have any children?
B: Yes, she has. She has two kids—a girl and a boy.

2 (live) A: do your grandparents Live in Sydney?
B: No, they dont. They Live in Ottawa.

3 (work) A: does your father work in Quito?
B: Yes, he does. He works for the government.

4 (like) A: does your cousin like hip-hop?
B: No, he doesnt He likes ... it at all.

CONVERSATION MODEL

2:06

A Read and listen to good news about a relationship.

A: What's new?

B: Actually, I have some good news. My sister just got engaged!

A: That's great. Congratulations!

B: Thanks!

A: So tell me about her fiancé.

B: Well, he works at PBM. He's an engineer.

Or bad news . . .

B: Actually, I have some bad news. My sister just got divorced.

A: I'm sorry to hear that. Is she OK?

B: Yes, she is. Thanks for asking.

2:07

B **Rhythm and intonation** Listen again and repeat. Then practice the Conversation Model with a partner.

NOW YOU CAN Report news about relationships

A **Notepadding** Imagine that you have good or bad news about someone in your extended family (or use real news). Write notes to plan a conversation.

Relationship to you:

What's the news?

Where does he / she live?

What does he / she do?

Other information:

good news	bad news
got married	got separated
got engaged	got divorced

B **Pair work** Personalize the Conversation Model to tell your partner your news. Then change roles.

A: What's new?

B: Actually, I have some .... news. My ....

A: ....

Don't stop!

- Ask yes / no questions.
  Is [she] ___? / Does [he] ___? / Do [they] ___?
- Use the simple present tense to say more.
  He lives ___. They have ___.
  She works ___. They don't have ___.

C **Change partners** Report other good or bad news.

GOAL Describe extended families

VOCABULARY Other family relationships

A 2:08 Read and listen. Then listen again and repeat.

1

Barry is my stepfather. He's my mother's second husband.

Gina is my stepmother. She's my father's second wife.

2

Jim is my stepbrother. His mother married my father.

Kayla is my stepsister.

3

Carl is my stepson. I married his father three years ago.

Tina is my stepdaughter. I married her mother when Tina was five.

4

Dana is my half-sister. We have the same mother, but different fathers.*

Rob's my half-brother.

*Half-brothers and half-sisters can also have the same father but different mothers.

B Pair work Ask your partner to find people in the photos.

"Who's Carl's stepmother?"

"Carl's stepmother is Gail."

C 2:09 **Listening comprehension** Listen to the speakers and infer the relationships. Use the Vocabulary to complete each statement. Listen again if necessary.

1 Her brother has three daughters.
2 Carol is his stepMother.
3 She calls her step mother "Mom."
4 Leo is his ....
5 Hank is her stepdaughter.

GRAMMAR The simple present tense—information questions: Review

What **do** your in-laws **do**?	What **does** your sister-in-law **do**?
Where **do** their grandparents **live**?	Where **does** your niece **live**?
When **do** you **visit** your aunt?	When **does** he **visit** his aunt?
How often **do** you **call** your nephew?	How often **does** she **call** her nephew?
How many cousins **do** they **have**?	How many cousins **does** he **have**?

Be careful! Who as subject:
Who **lives** in Hong Kong?
NOT Who ~~does live~~ in Hong Kong?

GRAMMAR BOOSTER ▸ p. 127
Information questions in the simple present tense:
- *Form*
- *Questions with Who*
- *Common errors*

A Find the grammar Look at the Photo Story on page 27 again. Find one information question in the simple present tense.

B Grammar practice Complete the conversations with the simple present tense.

1 A: .... nieces and nephews ....?
B: Three. My sister .... two girls, and my brother .... a boy.

2 A: My stepfather .... in a restaurant.
B: Really? .... he ....?
A: He's the chef and manager.

3 A: My sister .... with her family in Dublin.
B: Dublin? .... kids .... she have?
A: I have two nephews, both adopted.

4 A: .... your cousins live?
B: One .... in Thailand. And the other .... in Norway.
A: Wow! .... you see them?
B: They come home once a year.

5 A: Where .... your uncle ....?
B: He .... at the hospital around the corner.
A: .... your aunt .... there, too?
B: No, ... She's a homemaker.

CONVERSATION MODEL

A 2:10 Read and listen to people describing their families.

A: Do you come from a large family?
B: Not really. I have two brothers.
A: What about aunts and uncles?
B: Well, I have three aunts on my father's side. And on my mother's side, I have two aunts and three uncles.
A: That's pretty big!

B 2:11 **Rhythm and intonation** Listen again and repeat. Then practice the Conversation Model with a partner.

NOW YOU CAN Describe extended families

A Notepadding List your extended family relationships on the notepad.

On my father's side . . .	On my mother's side . . .

B Pair work Personalize the Conversation Model. Then change roles.

A: Do you come from a large family?
B: .... I have ....
A: What about ....?
B: Well, I have .... on my .... 's side. And ....
A: ....

Don't stop! Ask for more information.
Tell me about your [aunts].
Does she ___? / Do they ___?
Is she / Are they [single]?
What ___? Who ___?
Where ___? How often ___?
When ___? How many ___?

C Extension Now tell your classmates about your partner's family.

GOAL Compare people

BEFORE YOU LISTEN

A 2:12 **Vocabulary • *Similarities and differences*** Read and listen. Then listen again and repeat.

How are you alike?

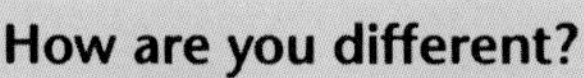

We look { **alike.** / **the same.** }

We wear **similar** / We like **the same kind of** } clothes.

We both / **Both of us** } like rock music.

How are you different?

We { **don't look alike.** / **look different.** }

We wear / We like } **different** clothes.

I like rock music, **but** { he likes classical. / he doesn't. }

B Pair work Find three similarities and three differences between you and your partner. On a separate sheet of paper, write six sentences describing the similarities and differences.

LISTENING COMPREHENSION

A 2:13 **Identify similarities and differences** Listen to Lucille Kennedy talk about herself and her sister, Laura. Check the statements that are true. Explain your answers.

Lucille and Laura . . .			
1	☐ look alike.	☐ look different.	
2	☐ like the same food.	☐ like different food.	
3	☐ like the same kinds of movies.	☐ like different kinds of movies.	
4	☐ sometimes wear the same clothes.	☐ never wear the same clothes.	
5	☐ like the same music.	☐ like different music.	
6	☐ have the same number of kids.	☐ have different numbers of kids.	
7	Lucille and Laura are ☐ twins.	☐ stepsisters.	☐ half-sisters.

2:14

B **Listen to take notes** Listen again for what Lucille says about these topics. On your notepad, use the Vocabulary to write sentences about how she and her sister are different.

favorite colors *They like different colors. Lucille likes . . .*

favorite colors	sports preferences
musical tastes	families

PRONUNCIATION *Blending sounds*

2:15

A Read and listen. Pay attention to the blended sounds in does she and does he. Then listen again and repeat.

1 Does she have any stepchildren? /dʌʃi/

2 How many stepchildren does she have? /dʌʃi/

3 Does he live near you? /dʌzi/

4 Where does he live? /dʌzi/

Now practice the questions on your own. Pay attention to blended sounds.

NOW YOU CAN Compare people

A **Notepadding** Choose someone in your extended family. On the notepad, write your similarities and differences. Use the Vocabulary from page 32.

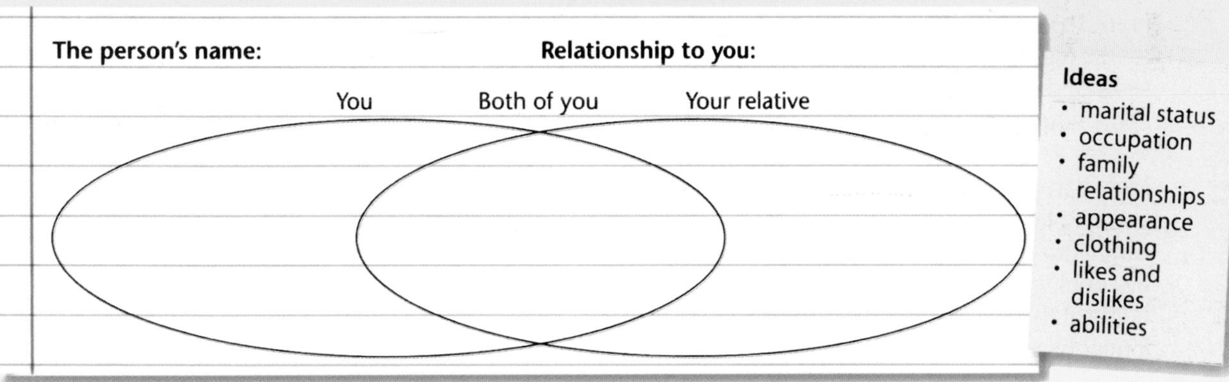

B **Pair work** Tell your partner about you and your relative. Use your notepad. Then compare other people in your families.

"My cousin and I are both single."

Be sure to recycle this language.

Similarities and differences
How are you alike?
How are you different?
Do you look alike?
Do you both ___ ?
Do you ___ the same ___ ?

For more information
How about ___ ?
Do you have any ___ ?
How old ___ ?
What does your ___ do?
Where does your ___ live?
How many ___ does your ___ have?

LESSON 4

GOAL Discuss family cultural traditions

BEFORE YOU READ

Warm-up In your opinion, how long should adult children live in their parents' homes?

READING

2:16 

Ask Mr. Dad with Armin Brott

Home | About "Ask Mr. Dad" | Ask a Question | About Armin Brott | Visit mrdad.com

When Adult Children Come Home

Q: ***My wife and I recently sent our last child off to college. We are ready to sell the house and travel, but our oldest daughter doesn't have a job and plans to move back home. What should we do?***

A: Most North Americans expect their children to move out of the house at eighteen. But that's changing. Today, more adult children are returning home to live. Some don't have jobs or can't pay for the high costs of housing. Some are recently separated or divorced. Most are single, but some come home with a wife, husband, or child, too.

Most parents are happy when their kids come back home to live. However, when a son or daughter can't find a job—or is recently divorced—there can be problems. And if their son or daughter is still at home at the age of thirty-five, many parents are no longer happy.

In your case, what if your daughter moves back home?

- Don't worry. If you and your daughter had a good relationship when she was younger, she'll be fine. Help her in any way you can. And it's OK to ask, "How long do you plan on staying?"
- Don't treat your daughter like a child. In our culture, adult children don't feel good about living at home, and they don't want to depend on their parents' help. Tell her you understand.
- Talk to your daughter as an adult. Have a discussion about paying for expenses and helping with household responsibilities and chores, such as kitchen cleanup and doing laundry. If you and your daughter talk and try to understand each other, everyone will be happier.

Ask Mr. Dad your question at askmrdad.com.

Source: mrdad.com

A Confirm facts Complete each statement.

1 The parents are worried because their daughter ....
   a wants to move into their home
   b wants to move away from their home
   c doesn't want to leave their home
   d doesn't want to come home

2 According to the article, most North Americans expect children to move out of their parents' home when they ....
   a reach the age of eighteen
   b finish college
   c find a job
   d get married

B Infer information Check all the correct answers, according to what Armin Brott says.

1 Check the reasons adult children are moving back home.
- ☐ They don't have jobs.
- ☐ They get divorced.
- ☐ They can't afford housing.
- ☐ They feel good about living with their parents.
- ☐ They want to depend on their parents.

2 What are Mr. Brott's suggestions to the father?
- ☐ to sell his house and go traveling
- ☐ to discuss chores at home
- ☐ to ask his daughter to find a job
- ☐ to try to understand his daughter
- ☐ to not worry too much about his daughter

On your *ActiveBook* Self-Study Disc:
Extra Reading Comprehension Questions

NOW YOU CAN Discuss family cultural traditions

A Frame your ideas Complete the survey about adult children in your country. Then compare answers with a partner.

Living At Home?

1 At what age do children usually leave home in your country?
- ☐ between 18 and 20
- ☐ between 21 and 25
- ☐ between 26 and 30
- ☐ over 30
- ☐ It depends on their marital status.

2 What are the reasons adult children usually leave home?
- ☐ They get a job.
- ☐ They get married.
- ☐ They go away to study.
- ☐ They don't want to depend on their parents.
- ☐ Other ____________________

3 How do parents feel when their adult children are living at home?
- ☐ They're very happy.
- ☐ They're very worried.
- ☐ They don't think about it.
- ☐ They don't want them to stay.
- ☐ Other ____________________

4 What do adult children usually do when they live at home?
- ☐ They help with the chores.
- ☐ They help pay for expenses.
- ☐ They look for a job.
- ☐ They look for a new place to live.
- ☐ Other ____________________

B Notepadding Write some similarities and differences between family cultural traditions in your country and those Armin Brott describes.

What's the same?	What's different?

C Group work Now imagine that you are speaking to a visitor to your country. Explain the family cultural traditions in your country about adult children living at home.

Text-mining (optional)
Underline language in the Reading on page 34 to use in the Group Work. For example:
"Most parents are happy when . . ."

Review

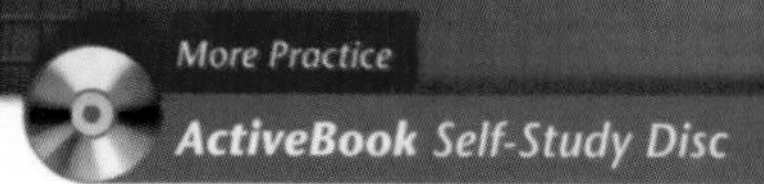

grammar · vocabulary · listening
reading · speaking · pronunciation

2:17

A **Listening comprehension** Listen to the people talking about their families. Check the box for family size for each speaker. Then listen again and write the number of children in each person's family.

		A big family	A small family	Number of children
1	Brenda	☐	☐	
2	Steven	☐	☐	
3	Leslie	☐	☐	
4	Jason	☐	☐	

B Complete the sentences with the correct word or phrase.

1 Larry doesn't have any brothers or sisters. He's an ....
2 Bob's brother is Ron. They have the same birth date. They are ....
3 Jun's brother has two daughters. They are Jun's ....
4 Eva is Alfonso's wife. Alfonso's parents are Eva's ....
5 Hariko's father has five nieces and nephews. They are Hariko's ....
6 Jill's father married Wendy's mother. Jill's father is Wendy's ....
7 Julie and Brett are divorced. Brett is Julie's ....
8 Teresa's mother has two brothers. They are Teresa's ....

C Complete the questions. Use the simple present tense.

1 A: Where ....?
B: My brother lives in Cuzco, Peru.

2 A: What ....?
B: My sister's a nurse.

3 A: How many ....?
B: I have two sons and a daughter.

4 A: ....?
B: Cousins? Yes, I do. I have seven.

5 A: Where ....?
B: My brother lives near me.

6 A: ....?
B: Children? Yes. My sister has two daughters.

2:18/2:19
Top Notch Pop
"An Only Child"
Lyrics p. 149

D **Writing** On a separate sheet of paper, compare two people in your family. Write about how they are similar and how they are different.

My brother and his wife are similar in some ways, but they are also very different . . .

WRITING BOOSTER ▸ p. 143
- *Combining sentences with <u>and</u> or <u>but</u>*
- *Guidance for Exercise D*

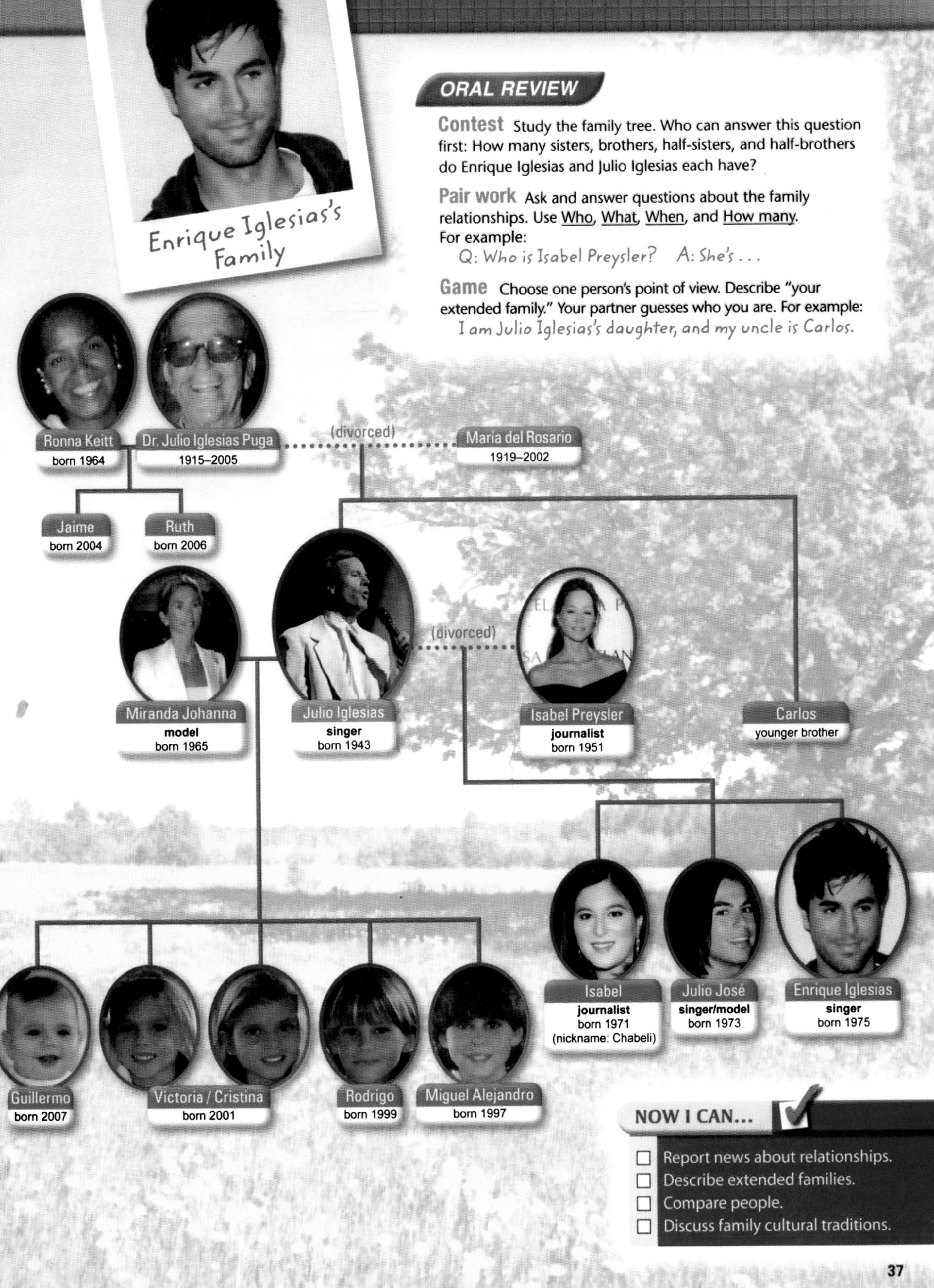

ORAL REVIEW

Contest Study the family tree. Who can answer this question first: How many sisters, brothers, half-sisters, and half-brothers do Enrique Iglesias and Julio Iglesias each have?

Pair work Ask and answer questions about the family relationships. Use Who, What, When, and How many. For example:

Q: Who is Isabel Preysler? *A: She's . . .*

Game Choose one person's point of view. Describe "your extended family." Your partner guesses who you are. For example:

I am Julio Iglesias's daughter, and my uncle is Carlos.

NOW I CAN...

- ☐ Report news about relationships.
- ☐ Describe extended families.
- ☐ Compare people.
- ☐ Discuss family cultural traditions.

UNIT 4

Food and Restaurants

Preview

GOALS After Unit 4, you will be able to:

1. Ask for a restaurant recommendation.
2. Order from a menu.
3. Speak to a server and pay for a meal.
4. Discuss food and health.

WORLD CAFÉ

Today's Specials

Appetizers

Potato soup Colombian Style

Fried squid with spicy tomato sauce

Salads

Mixed green salad

Tomato onion salad

Entrées

Brazilian steak

Grilled fish

Roast chicken

Desserts

Ice cream

Apple pie

German chocolate cake

Beverages

Coffee · Tea · Soft drinks · Fruit juice · Bottled water (still or sparkling)

A Read the menu. Circle the words that are new to you.

B 2:20 **Vocabulary** • *Parts of a meal* Listen and repeat.

C **Pair work** Which foods on the menu would you like to order? Are there any foods you wouldn't like to order? Compare tastes with a partner.

D **Notepadding** Write the name of at least one dish from your country for each category.

an appetizer	
a salad	
an entrée (main course)	
a dessert	
a beverage	

E 2:21 **Photo story** Read and listen to someone ordering food in a restaurant.

ENGLISH FOR TODAY'S WORLD
connecting people from different cultures and language backgrounds

Server:* Are you ready to order? Or do you need some more time?

Customer: I'm ready, thanks. I think I'll start with the potato soup. Then I'll have the roast chicken. What does that come with?

Server: It comes with a salad. And there's also a choice of vegetables. Tonight we have carrots or grilled tomatoes.

Customer: I'd like the carrots, please. Or, on second thought, maybe I'll have the tomatoes.

Server: Certainly. And anything to drink?

Customer: I'd like sparkling water, please. No ice.

*Server = waiter (man) or waitress (woman)

Server: Portuguese speaker

F Infer meaning Check the correct answers.

1 What does the customer order?
- ☐ an appetizer
- ☐ an entrée
- ☐ a dessert
- ☐ a beverage

2 What does the entrée come with?
- ☐ soup and salad
- ☐ salad and dessert
- ☐ carrots and grilled tomatoes
- ☐ salad and carrots or grilled tomatoes
- ☐ water

G Focus on language Use the menu from the World Café. Complete each statement.

1 I think I'll start with the ....

2 Then I'll have the ....

3 For my main course, I'd like the ....

4 For dessert, I'll have the ....

5 To drink, I'd like ....

Guest Check

Date	Table	Server	Check No. 2650

Tax

Total

H Pair work Read your statements to a partner. Your partner writes your order on the notepad. Then listen to and write your partner's statements.

LESSON 1

GOAL Ask for a restaurant recommendation

VOCABULARY Categories of food

A 2:22 Read and listen. Then listen again and repeat. Add another food to each category.

fruit

(1) apples (2) bananas
(3) grapes (4) oranges

mangoes ....

vegetables

(5) carrots (6) peppers
(7) broccoli (8) onions

....

meat

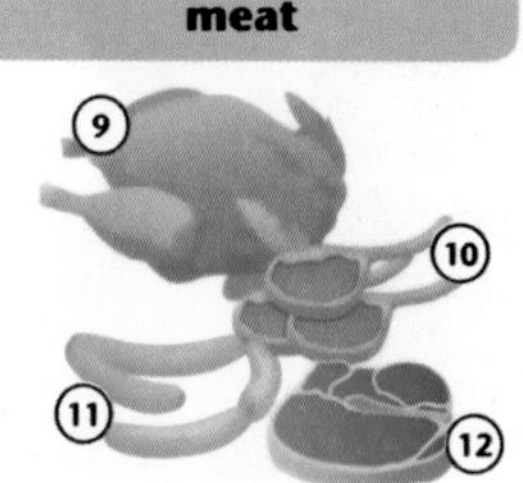

(9) chicken (10) lamb
(11) sausage (12) beef

....

seafood

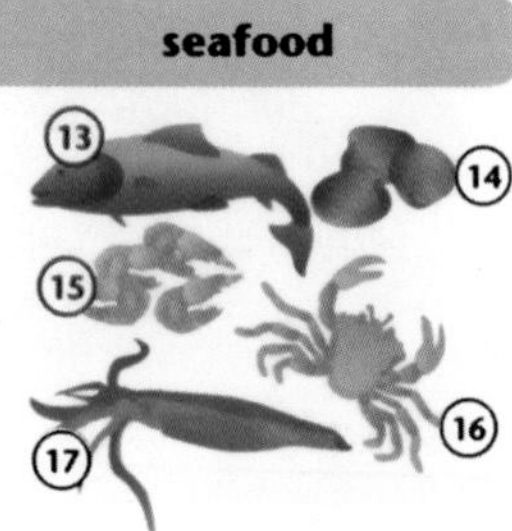

(13) fish (14) clams
(15) shrimp (16) crab
(17) squid ....

grains

(18) pasta (19) rice
(20) noodles (21) bread

....

dairy products

(22) butter (23) cheese
(24) milk (25) yogurt

....

oils

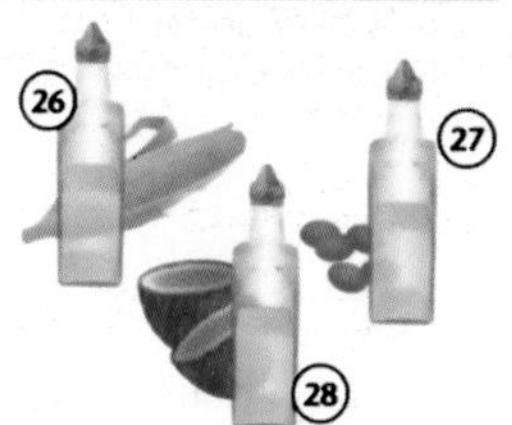

(26) corn oil (27) olive oil
(28) coconut oil

....

sweets

(29) candy (30) pie
(31) cake (32) cookies

....

B Expand the vocabulary How many foods can you create? Combine foods. Follow the example.

1 orange **juice** apple juice, mango juice ....
2 tomato onion **salad** ....
3 apple **pie** ....
4 **grilled** fish ....
5 **fried** squid ....
6 potato **soup** ....

GRAMMAR *There is* and *there are* with count and non-count nouns

Use there is with non-count nouns and singular count nouns.
Use there are with plural count nouns.

There's milk and an apple in the fridge.
There are oranges, too. But **there aren't** any vegetables.

Use there is with anything and nothing.

Is there anything to eat? (No, **there is** nothing.)
NOT ~~Are there~~ anything to eat?

Remember:

- Count nouns name things you can count. They are singular or plural.
- Non-count nouns name things you cannot count. They are not singular or plural.
- Don't use a, an, or a number with non-count nouns.
  rice NOT ~~a rice~~ NOT ~~rices~~

See page 122 for a more complete list of non-count nouns.

GRAMMAR BOOSTER ▸ p. 127

- *More on non-count nouns*
- *Expressing quantities*
- *How much / how many*
- *Spelling rules*

Grammar practice Complete each statement or question with a form of there is or there are.

1 .... apples in the fridge?

2 .... any cookies?

3 .... anything to eat in this house? I'm hungry.

4 .... eggs in the fridge. We could make an omelet.

5 I don't think .... any vegetables on the menu.

6 .... too much sugar in this coffee.

7 .... enough lettuce to make a salad?

8 .... any of that great cheese? I feel like having a grilled cheese sandwich.

CONVERSATION MODEL

2:23

A Read and listen to someone asking for a restaurant recommendation.

A: Could you recommend a restaurant for this evening?

B: Sure. What are you in the mood for?

A: I don't know. Maybe a sandwich. I'm not very hungry.

B: Actually, there's a great place nearby. It's called Tom's. Would you like directions?

2:24

B **Rhythm and intonation** Listen and repeat. Then practice the Conversation Model with a partner.

2:25

Degrees of hunger

– not very hungry
+ really hungry
+++ starving

NOW YOU CAN Ask for a restaurant recommendation

A Change the Conversation Model. Ask for a recommendation for today, tonight, dinner, breakfast, or lunch. Recommend a restaurant from the map. Then change roles.

A: Could you recommend a restaurant for ....?

B: .... What are you in the mood for?

A: I don't know. Maybe .... I'm ....

B: Actually, there's a great place nearby. It's called .... Would you like directions?

Don't stop!
Use the map and give directions to the restaurant you recommended.

Be sure to recycle this language.

Locations

around the corner	down the street from the ___
across the street	between ___ and ___
across from the ___	on the ___ side of the street

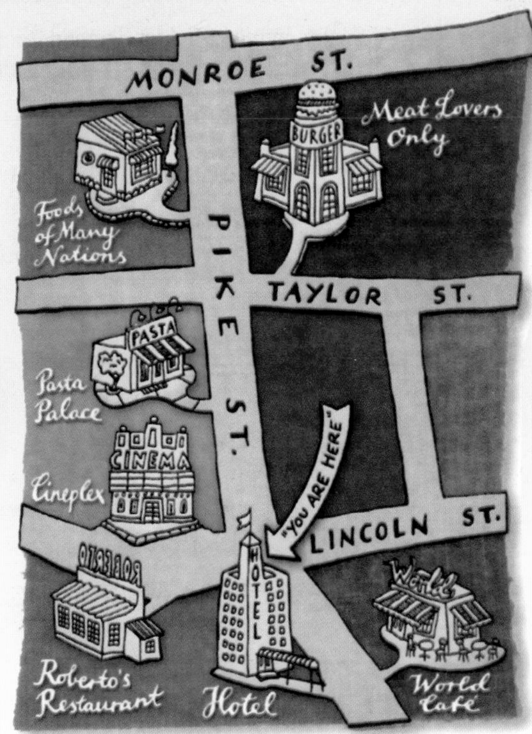

B **Change partners** Practice the conversation again. Talk about other foods and restaurants.

LESSON 2

GOAL Order from a menu

CONVERSATION MODEL

A 2:26 Read and listen to someone ordering dinner from a menu.

A: I'll have the pasta for my main course, please. What does that come with?

B: It comes with soup or a salad.

A: What kind of soup is there?

B: There's tomato soup or chicken soup.

A: I'd like the salad, please.

B: Certainly. And to drink?

A: Water, please.

B 2:27 **Rhythm and intonation** Listen again and repeat. Then practice the Conversation Model with a partner.

GRAMMAR *Definite article the*

Use the definite article the to name something a second time.

A: It comes with a salad.
B: OK. I'll have **the salad**.

Also use the to talk about something specific.

A: Would you like an appetizer? (not specific; general)
B: Yes. **The fried clams** sound delicious. (specific; they're on the menu)

A: I'm in the mood for seafood. (not specific; general)
B: Then I recommend **the grilled shrimp**. (also specific; they're on the menu)

Remember:
The indefinite articles are a and an.

a salad	**an** appetizer
a beverage	**an** entrée

GRAMMAR BOOSTER ▸ p. 129
• *Some and any*

A Find the grammar Look at the Photo Story on page 39 again. Explain why the customer uses the definite article the in the following sentences.

1 "I think I'll start with the potato soup."
2 "Then I'll have the roast chicken."
3 "I'd like the carrots, please."
4 " . . . maybe I'll have the tomatoes."

B Grammar practice Complete each conversation with a, an, or the.

1 A: What do you feel like eating tonight?
B: Well, ... seafood special sounds delicious.

2 A: I'm in the mood for .... really spicy dish.
B: Well, what about .... Thai chicken? Thai food is usually spicy.

3 A: There are two kinds of soup: chicken noodle and mixed vegetable.

B: I think I'd like .... chicken noodle. I'm not .... big vegetable fan.

4 A: What would you like for your main course? We have .... nice grilled chicken special on .... menu tonight.

B: That sounds good. I'll have .... chicken special.

PRONUNCIATION The

2:28

A Compare the pronunciation of the before consonant and vowel sounds. Read and listen. Then listen again and repeat.

/ə/ (before consonant sounds)	/i/ (before vowel sounds)
the chicken	the orange juice
the soup	the onion soup
the juice	the apple juice
the hot appetizer	the appetizer
the fried eggs	the eggs

B Write a check mark if the underlined word begins with a vowel sound.

☑ the egg salad	☐ the apple cake	☐ the clam soup
☐ the Chinese fried squid	☐ the ice cream	☐ the olive oil
☐ the tomato sauce	☐ the chocolate milk	☐ the grilled fish

C **Pair work** Now take turns saying each phrase. Be sure to use the correct pronunciation of the.

NOW YOU CAN Order from a menu

A With a partner, invent a restaurant. Give your restaurant a name. Write foods on the menu. Include two or more choices for each category.

B **Pair work** Use your menu to order food. Pay attention to count and non-count nouns and definite and indefinite articles. Then change roles.

A: I'll have .... for my main course, please. What does that come with?

B: It comes with ....

A: What kind of .... is there?

B: ....

A: I'd like ...., please.

B: Certainly. And to drink?

A: ...., please.

Don't stop!
- Order an appetizer or a soup.
- Order dessert.

C **Extension** Bring in a real menu from your favorite restaurant. Use it to practice the conversation. Change partners and menus and practice again.

Welcome to

____
(name of restaurant)

appetizers:
____

soup:
____

entrées:
____

beverages:
____

All entrées come with:
____

LESSON 3

GOAL Speak to a server and pay for a meal

BEFORE YOU LISTEN

2:29

Vocabulary • *Communicating with a waiter or waitress*
Read and listen. Then listen again and repeat.

LISTENING COMPREHENSION

2:30

A Listen to predict Listen to the conversations in a restaurant. Then listen again and predict the next thing you think the customer will say to the server. Explain your answers.

1 ☐ We'll take the check, please.
☐ Do you accept credit cards?
☐ We're ready to order.

2 ☐ This isn't what I ordered.
☐ We're ready to order.
☐ Is the tip included?

3 ☐ No, thanks. We'll take the check, please.
☐ Is the tip included?
☐ Do you accept credit cards?

4 ☐ Excuse me! This isn't what I ordered.
☐ Excuse me! We're ready to order.
☐ Excuse me! We'll take the check, please.

5 ☐ Excuse me!
☐ We'll start with the seafood soup, please.
☐ We'll take the check, please.

B Pair work Decide what to say to the server in each conversation. Then practice the conversation.

1 A: Oh, no! Have a look at this check!
B: I'm not sure we have enough money.
Excuse me! Do you accept credit cards?

2 A: Oh, no! They brought us onion soup.
We ordered the tomato soup.
B: You're right. Excuse me! ....

3 A: Oh, no! I left my money at home.
B: Excuse me! ....

4 A: We can't order dessert. We don't have time.
B: Right. Excuse me! ....

5 A: Do we need to leave a tip?
B: I'll ask. Excuse me! ....

6 A: Where's the waitress? I'm starving.
B: Excuse me! ....

NOW YOU CAN Speak to a server and pay for a meal

A Notepadding Plan your meal. Read the menu and choose what you'd like to order. Write your choice for each category.

appetizer	
soup	
salad	
main course	
beverage	
dessert	

Parkview Restaurant

Appetizers
Crab cakes
Mini cheese pies
Mixed grilled vegetables

Soup
Spicy shrimp
Chicken and rice
French onion

Salads
Tomato pepper
Green bean
Carrot

Entrées
Roast beef
Fried fish
Pasta with clam sauce
Choice of Vegetables: Broccoli, Grilled tomatoes, Potatoes (any style)

Desserts
Ice cream sandwiches
Banana cake
Chocolate pie
Mixed fruit salad
Fruit and cheese plate

All entrées include bread, soup or salad, vegetable, coffee or tea

B Group work Now form groups of diners and servers at tables. Discuss the menu. Speak to the server. Order and pay for the meal.

Be sure to recycle this language.

Discuss food
What are you in the mood for?
I'm in the mood for ___ .
There's ___ on the menu.
The ___ sound(s) delicious.
What about ___ ?
This isn't what I ordered.

Serve food
Are you ready to order?
Do you need more time?
That comes with ___ .
Would you like ___ ?
Anything to drink?
And to drink?
And for your [entrée]?

Order food
Excuse me!
I'm / We're ready.
I'd like to start with ___ .
I think I'll have ___ .
And then I'll have ___ .
Does that come with ___ ?
What does that come with?
What kind of ___ is there?

Pay for food
I'll / We'll take the check, please.
Is the tip included?
Do you accept credit cards?

LESSON 4

GOAL Discuss food and health

BEFORE YOU READ

A 2:31 **Vocabulary • *Adjectives to describe the healthfulness of food*** Read and listen. Then listen again and repeat.

healthy / healthful is good for you

unhealthy / unhealthful is bad for you

fatty / high-fat contains a lot of oil

salty contains a lot of salt

sweet contains a lot of sugar

high-calorie can make you fat or overweight

low-calorie is not going to make you fat

B **Warm-up** Do you like to eat at fast-food restaurants? Is it possible to get healthy food there? Use the Vocabulary.

READING

2:32 

File Edit View History Bookmarks Tools Help

Get Smart! *Eating on the go*

Home | Eating on the go

We know a daily diet of fast food can be bad for us. But fast food is quick and easy, and when we're on the go, it's sometimes a necessary choice. So here are some tips for fast-food fans:

Eat more "veggies."

- **Choose the chicken.** Have chicken rather than red meat. When in doubt, order the grilled chicken—not the fried.
- **Go light on the sauce.** Mayo, salad dressings, and other sauces are loaded with calories. Cut down on them, or cut them out altogether!

Cut down on mayo.

- **Fill up on veggies.** Ask for tomato, lettuce, onion, or other veggies on your sandwich. These low-calorie choices can help you avoid fries and other high-calorie options.

Skip the fries.

- **Go for the regular size,** not the extra-large. Super-size portions can super-size YOU.
- **Skip the sides entirely.** Eating a burger by itself is often enough. If you need a side order of something, consider a fruit cup or a side salad, instead of those fatty, salty french fries. Most fast-food restaurants offer those healthy options now.

Get a side salad.

- **Finally, treat yourself.** When you just have to have something sweet, opt for some delicious low-fat frozen yogurt or fruit ices rather than ice cream or cookies. You won't miss the calories a bit!

Source: fruitsandveggiesmatter.gov

A Understand from context Find the following words and phrases in the Reading and match them with their meanings. Then, on a separate sheet of paper, use the words to write your own sentences.

....	**1** "veggies"	**a** the amount you eat at one time
....	**2** "side order"	**b** not choose
....	**3** "go for"	**c** vegetables
....	**4** "skip" or "avoid"	**d** choice
....	**5** "portion"	**e** something you eat with your main course
....	**6** "option"	**f** choose

B Infer information Which tips on the website can help you cut down on calories? fat? salt? sugar? Explain how.

On your *ActiveBook* Self-Study Disk:
Extra Reading Comprehension Questions

NOW YOU CAN Discuss food and health

"French fries are not healthy. They're too fatty."

"I agree."

A Frame your ideas Write a ✓ next to the foods you think are healthy. Write an X next to the foods you think are not. Then discuss your answers with a partner. Explain why some of the foods are unhealthy.

- ☑ rice
- ☐ french fries
- ☑ hot peppers
- ☑ ice cream
- ☐ snacks: nuts, chips
- ☑ chicken
- ☑ salad
- ☑ pasta with sauce

B Notepadding List other foods and drinks you think are good for you and bad for you.

Healthy foods	Unhealthy foods
oranges	*salty foods, like potato chips*

C Discussion Now discuss food and health with your class. Suggest healthy eating tips. Use your lists.

Be sure to recycle this language.

Categories of foods		Adjectives	Verbs
grains	meat	healthy / unhealthy	skip / avoid / cut out
seafood	sweets	good / bad for you	go light on / cut down on
dairy products	fruit	high-calorie / low-calorie	fill up on
vegetables	oils	fatty / salty / sweet / spicy	

Text-mining (optional)
Underline more language in the Reading on page 46 to use in the Discussion. For example:
"Have ___ rather than ___."

Review

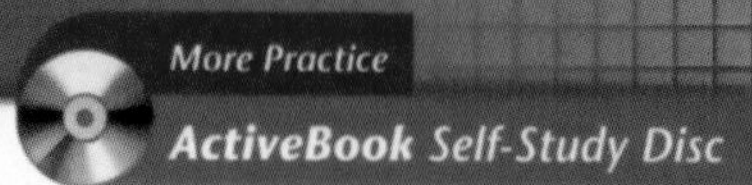

grammar · vocabulary · listening
reading · speaking · pronunciation

A 2:33 **Listening comprehension** Listen to the conversations. Where are the people? Choose at home or in a restaurant. Then predict what each person will say next. Listen again and complete the statements.

1 The man and woman are (at home / in a restaurant).
I think he's going to ask, "Does dessert .... with my ....?"

2 Caroline and her mom are (at home / in a restaurant).
Her mom is probably going to say, "But Caroline, ... are really ...."

3 The man and woman are (at home / in a restaurant).
It's possible that he's going to say, ".................... the grilled ...."

4 The couple is (at home / in a restaurant).
It's possible that she's going to say, "Terrific! Let's .... an omelet and a salad. I'm really ....!"

B Write examples of foods for each description below.

Spicy foods	Salty foods	Sweet foods	Fatty foods

C Write four questions you can ask a waiter or a waitress.

1 ....
2 ....
3 ....
4 ....

2:34/2:35 **Top Notch Pop** "The World Café" Lyrics p. 149

D Complete each sentence with a form of there is or there are.

1 .... too much pepper in the soup.
2 I hope .... not too much sugar in the cake. Sugar isn't good for you.
3 Excuse me. I'm looking for a restaurant. .... any good restaurants in the neighborhood?
4 .... any low-fat desserts on the menu?
5 .... an inexpensive restaurant nearby?
6 You should eat some fruit. .... some nice oranges on the kitchen table.
7 .... enough cheese in the fridge for two sandwiches?
8 I'm in the mood for soup. What kind of soup .... on the menu?

E **Writing** On a separate sheet of paper, write a short article for a travel newsletter. Write at least five sentences about foods in your country. Write more if you can.

In my country we eat a lot of vegetables. Vegetable soup is a very typical appetizer . . .

WRITING BOOSTER ▸ p. 143
- *Connecting words and ideas: and, in addition*
- *Guidance for Exercise E*

ORAL REVIEW
Pair work Create conversations for the people in Pictures 1, 2, and 3. For example:
A: Can I help you?
B: Could you recommend a restaurant for . . . ?
Contest Form teams. Each team takes turns making statements about the foods in Picture 4 with there is or there are. (Teams get one point for each correct statement.)
1
2
3
4
NOW I CAN...
Ask for a restaurant recommendation.
Order from a menu.
Speak to a server and pay for a meal.
Discuss food and health.

UNIT 5

Technology and You

Preview

GOALS After Unit 5, you will be able to:

1. Suggest a brand or model.
2. Express frustration and sympathy.
3. Describe features of products.
4. Complain when things don't work.

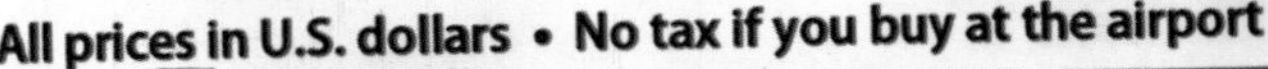

A 3:02 **Vocabulary • *Electronics*** Listen and repeat.

a laptop (computer)	a digital camera
a desktop (computer)	headphones
an earphone	a projector
a GPS	an MP3 player
a DVD player	a camcorder
a flash drive	speakers

B Discussion Choose a product from the ad that you would like in order to replace an old one. Discuss the reasons. Use this vocabulary or your own ideas.

3:03 **Replacing products**

broken doesn't work
obsolete hard to use because the technology is old
up-to-date uses new or recent technology
defective not good; badly designed and/or manufactured

C 3:04 Photo story Read and listen to a conversation about a product that's not working.

Don: This printer's driving me crazy! It's on the blink again.

Erin: What's wrong with it?

Don: What isn't wrong with it? It's an absolute lemon.

Erin: No, seriously, what's the problem?

Don: Well, first off, the thing's an antique. It's ten years old.

Erin: OK. And . . . ?

Don: And it's so slow. It takes hours to print! And now it won't print at all!

Erin: Well, that is a problem. Maybe it's fixable. Let me have a look.

Don: Don't bother. It's not worth it. The thing's obsolete, anyway. It's not wireless, it has no scanner, it can't photocopy . . .

Erin: Sounds like you're ready for an upgrade. Airport Electronics is having a sale. Let's get you something more up-to-date!

D Focus on language Find the following sentences and phrases in the Photo Story. Choose the statement that is closer in meaning to each sentence.

1 "This printer's driving me crazy!"
- **a** I love this printer!
- **b** I hate this printer!

2 "It's on the blink again."
- **a** The printer has a problem.
- **b** The printer is OK.

3 "It's an absolute lemon."
- **a** It's very bad.
- **b** It's very good.

4 ". . . the thing's an antique."
- **a** It's very new.
- **b** It's very old.

5 "Don't bother. It's not worth it."
- **a** I don't want to fix the printer.
- **b** I want to fix the printer.

6 ". . . you're ready for an upgrade."
- **a** You need a new printer.
- **b** Someone needs to fix your printer.

E Pair work Make a list of five electronic products that are necessary for your life. Put them in order from most important (1) to least important (5). Compare lists with a partner. Explain why each product is necessary for you.

"I can't live without a laptop. I use it at work and at home . . ."

	Product	Why necessary?
1		
2		
3		
4		
5		

LESSON 1

GOAL Suggest a brand or model

CONVERSATION MODEL

3:05
A Read and listen to someone suggesting a brand and a model.

A: Hey, Lisa. What are you doing?

B: I'm online. I'm looking for a flat screen TV. Any suggestions?

A: What about a Clarion? I hear the LP 10 is great. And it's inexpensive.

B: Really?

A: Yes. You know, I'm going shopping later. Would you like to come along?

3:07
Positive descriptions
pretty good ☺
great ☺☺
terrific ☺☺☺
awesome ☺☺☺☺

3:06
B Rhythm and intonation Listen again and repeat. Then practice the Conversation Model with a partner.

GRAMMAR *The present continuous: Review*

I / You / We / They	**are shopping.** / **aren't shopping.**	He / She	**is shopping.** / **isn't shopping.**

Use the present continuous for actions in progress now and for future plans.

Actions in progress
A: What **are** you **doing** right now?
B: I'**m looking** for a laptop.

Future plans
A: What **are** you **doing** tomorrow?
B: I'**m buying** a digital camera.

Questions
Are you **looking** for a cell phone? (Yes, I am. / No, I'm not.)
Are they **buying** a GPS? (Yes, they are. / No, they're not.)
Is he **using** the computer? (Yes, he is. / No, he's not.)
Where **are** you **going**? (To Technoland.)
Who'**s buying** the new cell phone? (My wife.)

GRAMMAR BOOSTER ▸ p. 130
The present continuous:
- *Spelling rules*
- *Form and usage rules*

Understand the grammar Write now next to the statements or questions where the present continuous describes an action in progress. Write future next to those that describe a future plan.

future **1** What are you doing this weekend?
.... **2** I'm busy this morning. I'm answering e-mails.
.... **3** He's leaving in ten minutes. Hurry!
.... **4** Josh isn't home. He's shopping for a laptop.
.... **5** They're eating with us on Friday.
.... **6** The printer's not working again.

PRONUNCIATION *Intonation of questions*

3:08
Listen and check for rising or falling intonation. Then take turns saying each question.

↗ ☐ ↘ ☐ **1** What are you doing?
↗ ☐ ↘ ☐ **2** Are you buying a computer?
↗ ☐ ↘ ☐ **3** What time are you going?
↗ ☐ ↘ ☐ **4** Is she looking for a new printer?

VOCABULARY More electronics

A 3:09 Read and listen. Then listen again and repeat.

a smart phone

a cell phone / a mobile phone

a scanner

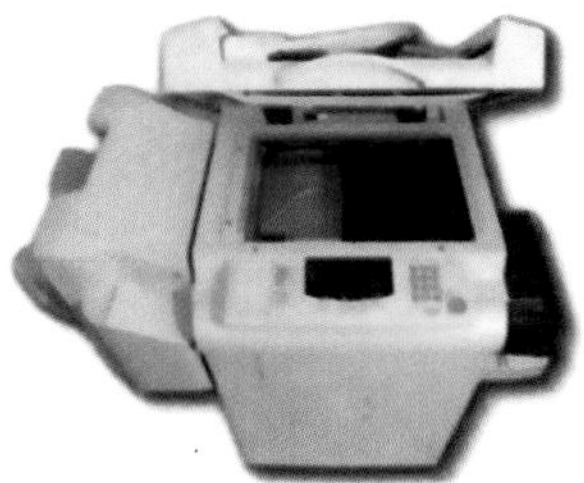
a photocopier

a fax machine

B Integrated practice Complete each conversation with an electronic product from pages 50–53 and the present continuous.

1 A: .... to Electronica tomorrow?
Marian / go
B: Yes. .... for a new ....
she / shop
The old one is broken, and she listens to music while she's exercising.

2 A: Why .... a ....?
Ann / get
B: She sends a lot of e-mails to her friends, and
....
her old one / not work

3 A: Can I use your ....?
B: Sure. But just a minute. Right now ....
I / use
it to move a file from my laptop to my desktop.

4 A: .... a new presentation, and
Sue / prepare
she wants to use these pictures.
B: She's welcome to use my ....
It's really great.

5 A: Is it possible to use your .... for my son's birthday party?
B: Sure. What day? .... it tomorrow at
I / use
the school play. After that, you can have it.

6 A: What ....?
your parents / watch
B: A music video. Now that they have a
........................, they watch all day!

NOW YOU CAN Suggest a brand or model

A Pair work Change the Conversation Model, using these ads or ads from a newspaper or online store. Then change roles.

A: I'm looking for .... Any suggestions?
B: What about .... ? I hear the .... is .... And it's ....
A: Really?
B: Yes. You know, I'm going shopping .... Would you like to come along?

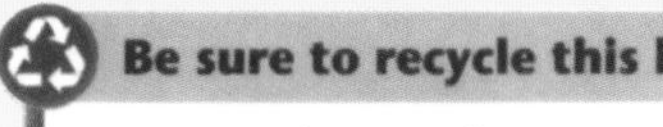

Are you free ___?
I'd love to go, but I ___.
I'm sorry, but I'm not free ___.

Don't stop!
Accept or decline the invitation.

B Change partners Discuss other products and suggest other brands or models.

LESSON 2

GOAL Express frustration and sympathy

CONVERSATION MODEL

A 3:10 Read and listen to people expressing frustration and sympathy.

A: Hi, Ed. How's it going?

B: Fine, thanks. But my microwave's not working again.

A: Again? I'm sorry to hear that. What brand is it?

B: A Quickpoint. It's a piece of junk.

B 3:11 **Rhythm and intonation** Listen again and repeat. Then practice the Conversation Model with a partner.

3:12 **Ways to sympathize**

I'm sorry to hear that.
That's too bad.
That's a shame.
Oh, no!

3:13 **Negative descriptions**

a piece of junk	awful
pretty bad	horrible
terrible	a lemon

VOCABULARY *Household appliances and machines*

A 3:14 Read and listen. Then listen again and repeat.

1 a food processor
2 a hair dryer 
3 a pressure cooker 
4 a dishwasher 
5 a coffee maker 
6 a rice cooker 
7 a fan 
8 a stove 
9 an oven
10 a juicer  
11 a washing machine
12 a dryer
13 a blender
14 a freezer
15 a refrigerator / a fridge
16 an air-conditioner 
17 a vacuum cleaner

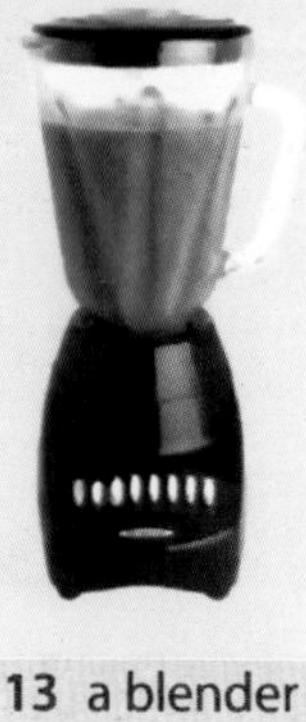

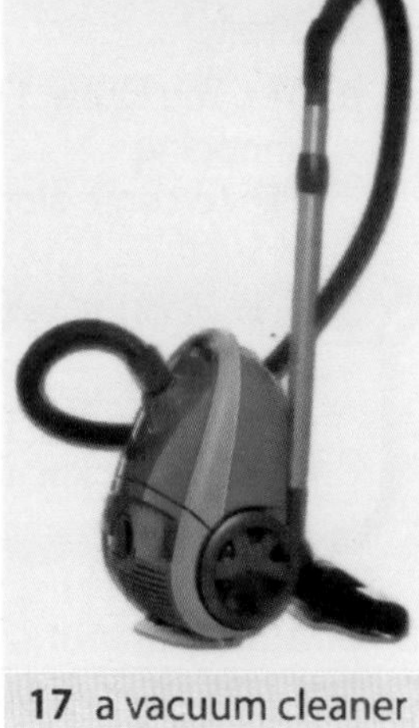

B Classify the Vocabulary by purpose. Write examples of appliances in each category.

For cleaning or washing	For food preparation	For cooking	For storage

C 3:15 **Listen to predict** Listen and write the name of the appliance. Then listen again and predict what the other person will say. Check the box.

1 appliance: ....
- ☐ Is it fixable?
- ☐ Sure. No problem.

2 appliance: ....
- ☐ It's an air-conditioner.
- ☐ It's a Cool Wave.

3 appliance: ....
- ☐ It's not working? That's a shame.
- ☐ About thirty, I think.

4 appliance: ....
- ☐ Oops! Sorry about that.
- ☐ Sounds great!

5 appliance: ....
- ☐ Just use a little more water.
- ☐ I think the machine is defective.

6 appliance: ....
- ☐ Yeah. I'm so glad I bought it!
- ☐ I think it's time for an upgrade.

7 appliance: ....
- ☐ It's a lemon.
- ☐ Wow. That sounds great.

8 appliance: ....
- ☐ I'm sorry to hear that.
- ☐ Sure. Just a second.

NOW YOU CAN Express frustration and sympathy

A **Notepadding** Think of five products and brands that don't work well. Write them on the notepad.

	Product	Brand
1	*a hair dryer*	*Beautiful Hair*

	Product	Brand
1		
2		
3		
4		
5		

B **Pair work** Change the Conversation Model. Use your own products and brands. Express frustration and sympathy. Use the negative descriptions vocabulary from page 54. Then change roles.

A: Hi, ... How's it going?

B: .... But my ....'s not working again.

A: Again? .... What brand is it?

B: .... It's ....

C **Change partners** Express frustration about other products and brands.

GOAL Describe features of products

BEFORE YOU READ

Warm-up What kinds of features are important to you in a new product?

READING

3:16 

PRO MUSICA

More than a radio, more than a CD player, more than an MP3 player—the Pro Musica is the first complete music system for your entire life. The innovative, all-in-one Pro Musica fills all the rooms of your house with beautiful music from just one source.

It replaces everything else you listen to. MP3 players, radios, and CD players are a thing of the past. And the whole family can be listening to their favorite music in every room at the same time.

Program the Pro Musica to play Metallica in the kitchen and Brahms in the bedroom. Listen with the portable wireless speakers or on your innovative wireless earbuds. You and your spouse can even be listening to two different things in the very same room at the same time. The sky's the limit!

And even better—you can take the Pro Musica's remote and wireless speakers with you anywhere—to the office, to your friend's house for a party, or even to the beach. Play anything, anywhere.

The Pro Musica wireless remote— Battery operated and easy to use.

The Pro Musica wireless speakers— Place them anywhere.

The Pro Musica wireless earbuds— Move around as you listen.

FEATURES

- **IT'S CONVENIENT.** Everything you need is built into the system so you can enjoy your music all from one source—and with only one simple-to-use remote control.
- **IT'S POPULAR.** The Pro Musica is now used by more households than any other home music system.
- **IT'S PORTABLE.** The remote is small and easy to carry. It comes with its own battery pack, so you can take it with you anywhere.
- **IT'S AFFORDABLE.** One Pro Musica system costs much less than the many CD players, radios, etc. that most people have to buy to have music in their lives.
- **IT'S GUARANTEED.** Use Pro Musica for a full year. If for any reason you are unhappy with the product, just return it for a full refund.

A Understand from context Choose one of the features to complete each statement.

1 A product that's easy to move from one place to another is ....
2 A product that's easy to use is ....
3 A product that you can send back to the store because you don't like it is ....
4 A product that a lot of people like and buy is ....
5 A product that doesn't cost too much for most people is ....

Features
guaranteed
popular
portable
affordable
convenient

B Activate language from a text Would you buy the Pro Musica? Explain your answer. Use the features vocabulary and your own ideas.

C 3:17 **Listening comprehension** Listen to the radio advertisements for some crazy gadgets. Check all the adjectives that describe each product.

gadget /'gædʒɪt/ n.
a small tool or machine that makes a particular job easier

Longman Dictionary of American English

1 "The Sleeper"

- ☐ convenient
- ☐ popular
- ☐ portable
- ☐ affordable

2 "Cool as a Cucumber"

- ☐ convenient
- ☐ popular
- ☐ portable
- ☐ affordable

3 "The Scribbler"

- ☐ guaranteed
- ☐ convenient
- ☐ affordable
- ☐ popular

D 3:18 **Pair work** Choose one of the three gadgets. Listen again and take notes on a separate sheet of paper. Then try to convince your partner to buy the product. Use the features vocabulary from the Reading on page 56.

On your *ActiveBook* Self-Study Disc:
Extra Reading Comprehension Questions

NOW YOU CAN Describe features of products

A Notepadding Choose one good product that you own and one bad product (appliances, electronic products, gadgets, etc.). Write the good and bad features on the notepad.

Product	Brand	Features
scanner	Blue Bird	obsolete
MP3 player	Vista	affordable / up-to-date

Product	Brand	Features

B Discussion Describe the features of your products. Tell your classmates about all the good and bad features.

"I don't recommend the Blue Bird scanner. It's obsolete."

"You should buy the new Vista MP3 player. It's affordable and up-to-date."

Be sure to recycle this language.

Negative descriptions
awful
broken
defective
horrible
not fixable
obsolete
on the blink
slow
terrible
an antique
a lemon
a piece of junk
drives me crazy

Positive descriptions
great
terrific
awesome
fast
popular
guaranteed
affordable
convenient
pretty good
up-to-date

Ways to sympathize
I'm sorry to hear that.
That's too bad.
That's a shame.
Oh, no!
Maybe it's fixable.
You're ready for an upgrade.

GOAL Complain when things don't work

BEFORE YOU LISTEN

A 3:19 **Vocabulary • *Ways to state a problem*** Read and listen. Then listen again and repeat.

The window **won't open / close.**

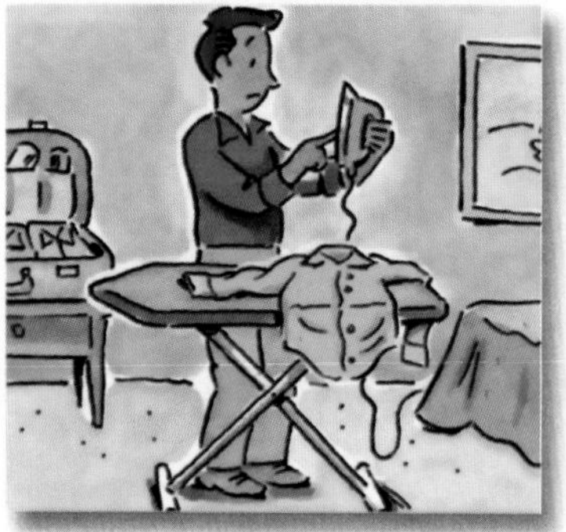
The iron **won't turn on.**

The air-conditioning **won't turn off.**

The fridge is **making a funny sound.**

The toilet **won't flush.**

The sink **is clogged.**

B Write the names of machines, appliances, and gadgets that sometimes . . .

1 won't open or close. ....

2 won't turn on or off. ....

3 make a funny sound. ....

LISTENING COMPREHENSION

A 3:20 **Listen for details** Listen to the conversations. Write the room number for each complaint. Then listen again and write another problem for each room.

GUEST COMPLAINT LOG

ROOM	PROBLEM	OTHER PROBLEMS?
203	*The toilet won't stop flushing.*	
	The fridge isn't working.	
	The sink is clogged.	

B Discussion Which problems on the guest complaint log are serious? Which are not serious? Explain your reasons.

"It's serious when the sink is clogged. Water on the floor is very bad."

NOW YOU CAN Complain when things don't work

A Notepadding Find and circle all the problems in the hotel. Write the problems on the notepad.

Room / place	Problem(s)

B Pair work Create conversations between the hotel guests and the front desk clerk. Based on the pictures, complain about things that don't work.

"Hello. Front desk. Can I help you?"

"I'm in the elevator. It's not working."

"I'll send someone right away."

Be sure to recycle this language.

Telephone language
Hello?
This room ___ .
Can I call you back?
Bye.

State a problem
___ won't open / close.
___ won't turn on / off.
___ won't flush / stop flushing.
___ isn't working.
___ is clogged.
___ is making a funny sound.
___ is driving me crazy.

Respond
What's the problem?
I'm sorry to hear that.
Oh, no!
Well, that <u>is</u> a problem.

Review

More Practice
ActiveBook *Self-Study Disc*
grammar • vocabulary • listening
reading • speaking • pronunciation

3:21

A **Listening comprehension** Listen to the conversations about problems with products and appliances. Write a sentence to describe each problem.

Example: *The fan won't turn on.*

1 ....

2 ....

3 ....

4 ....

3:22/3:23
Top Notch Pop
"It's Not Working Again"
Lyrics p. 149

B Complete each conversation with a question in the present continuous. (It's possible to write more than one question.)

1 A: Where .... tomorrow?
B: We're going to My Electronics World. Want to come along?

2 A: Are you .... a new camera?
B: Yes. Our old camera is obsolete. It's not digital.

3 A: When ....?
B: He's getting a smart phone for his birthday.

4 A: What ....?
B: Tomorrow? We're fixing our old printer.

5 A: What ....?
B: Right now? We're eating dinner.

C Complete each statement. Circle the correct word or phrase.

1 This new toilet is (defective / portable). It doesn't flush.

2 I think my TV is (affordable / broken). I hope it's fixable.

3 Your computer is probably (obsolete / up-to-date). You should get a new one.

4 This scanner is really a piece of junk. I think we should get (an upgrade / a lemon).

D Classify products, appliances, and gadgets on the following chart. Write at least three in each category. (Some products may go in more than one category.)

Machines that are:						
Portable	Popular	Convenient	Affordable	Good for communication	Good for entertainment	Good for cooking
					MP3 player	

E **Writing** On a separate sheet of paper, write a paragraph describing a product, appliance, or gadget that you use. It can be a good product or a bad one.

I have a Hot Spot dishwasher and . . .

WRITING BOOSTER ▸ p. 144
- *Placement of adjectives*
- *Guidance for Exercise E*

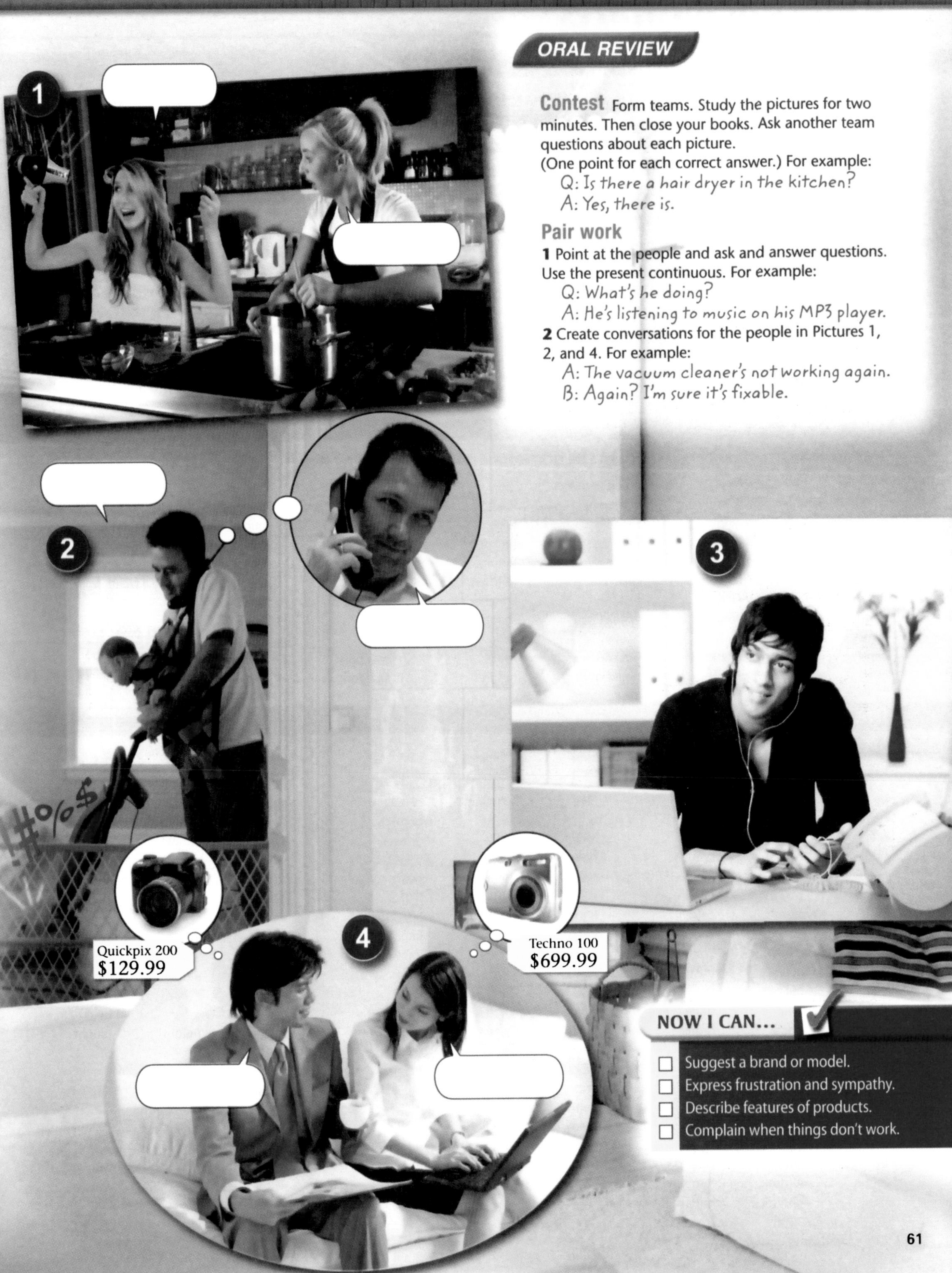

ORAL REVIEW

Contest Form teams. Study the pictures for two minutes. Then close your books. Ask another team questions about each picture.
(One point for each correct answer.) For example:

Q: Is there a hair dryer in the kitchen?
A: Yes, there is.

Pair work

1 Point at the people and ask and answer questions. Use the present continuous. For example:

Q: What's he doing?
A: He's listening to music on his MP3 player.

2 Create conversations for the people in Pictures 1, 2, and 4. For example:

A: The vacuum cleaner's not working again.
B: Again? I'm sure it's fixable.

NOW I CAN...

- ☐ Suggest a brand or model.
- ☐ Express frustration and sympathy.
- ☐ Describe features of products.
- ☐ Complain when things don't work.

Reference Charts

Countries and nationalities

Country	Nationality
Argentina	Argentinean / Argentine
Australia	Australian
Belgium	Belgian
Bolivia	Bolivian
Brazil	Brazilian
Canada	Canadian
Chile	Chilean
China	Chinese
Colombia	Colombian
Costa Rica	Costa Rican
Ecuador	Ecuadorian
Egypt	Egyptian
El Salvador	Salvadorean
France	French
Germany	German
Greece	Greek
Guatemala	Guatemalan
Holland	Dutch
Honduras	Honduran
Hungary	Hungarian
India	Indian
Indonesia	Indonesian
Ireland	Irish
Italy	Italian
Japan	Japanese
Korea	Korean
Lebanon	Lebanese
Malaysia	Malaysian
Mexico	Mexican
Nicaragua	Nicaraguan
Panama	Panamanian
Paraguay	Paraguayan
Peru	Peruvian
Poland	Polish
Portugal	Portuguese
Russia	Russian
Saudi Arabia	Saudi / Saudi Arabian
Spain	Spanish
Sweden	Swedish
Switzerland	Swiss
Taiwan	Chinese
Thailand	Thai
Turkey	Turkish
the United Kingdom	British
the United States	American
Uruguay	Uruguayan
Venezuela	Venezuelan
Vietnam	Vietnamese

Non-count nouns

This list is an at-a-glance reference to the non-count nouns used in *Top Notch 1*.

aerobics
air-conditioning
basketball
beef
bike riding
bread
broccoli
butter
cake
candy
cash
cheese
chicken
clothing
coffee
crab
culture
dancing
dessert
dinner
electronics
English
entertainment
fish
food
fruit
garlic
golf
health
history
hosiery
hot sauce
housework
ice
ice cream
juice
junk food
lamb
lettuce
lingerie
meat
milk
music
nature
oil
outerwear
pasta
pepper
pie
rice
running
salad
salt
sausage
seafood
service
shopping
shrimp
sightseeing
skydiving
sleepwear
soccer
soup
squid
swimming
tennis
traffic
transportation
TV
walking
water
weather
wildlife
yogurt

Irregular verbs

base form	simple past	past participle
be	was / were	been
begin	began	begun
break	broke	broken
bring	brought	brought
build	built	built
buy	bought	bought
catch	caught	caught
choose	chose	chosen
come	came	come
cost	cost	cost
cut	cut	cut
do	did	done
drink	drank	drunk
drive	drove	driven
eat	ate	eaten
fall	fell	fallen
feel	felt	felt
find	found	found
fit	fit	fit
fly	flew	flown
forget	forgot	forgotten
get	got	gotten
give	gave	given
go	went	gone
grow	grew	grown
have	had	had
hear	heard	heard
hit	hit	hit
hurt	hurt	hurt
keep	kept	kept
know	knew	known
leave	left	left
lose	lost	lost
make	made	made
mean	meant	meant
meet	met	met
pay	paid	paid
put	put	put
quit	quit	quit
read	read	read
ride	rode	ridden
run	ran	run
say	said	said
see	saw	seen
sell	sold	sold
send	sent	sent
shake	shook	shaken
sing	sang	sung
sit	sat	sat
sleep	slept	slept
speak	spoke	spoken
spend	spent	spent
stand	stood	stood
steal	stole	stolen
swim	swam	swum
take	took	taken
teach	taught	taught
tell	told	told
think	thought	thought
throw	threw	thrown
understand	understood	understood
wake up	woke up	woken up
wear	wore	worn
win	won	won
write	wrote	written

TOP NOTCH
1A
Grammar Booster

Grammar Booster

The Grammar Booster is optional. It is not required for the achievement tests in the *Top Notch Complete Assessment Package*. If you use the Grammar Booster, there are extra exercises in the Workbook in a separate labeled Grammar Booster section.

UNIT 1 *Lesson 1*

Information questions with be: usage and form

Use Who to ask about people, What to ask about things, Where to ask about places, and How old to ask about age.

singular nouns	plural nouns
Who**'s** your teacher?	Who **are** the new students?
What**'s** your name?	What **are** their names?
Where**'s** your father from?	Where **are** your classmates from?
How old **is** your sister?	How old **are** your children?

A Choose an answer for each question.

___ **1** What's your name?
___ **2** Where is she from?
___ **3** Where's her father from?
___ **4** Who is Bernard Udall?
___ **5** How old are your cousins?

a Scotland, actually. She's British.
b He's the CEO of BRC Incorporated.
c Kim's father? Seoul, I think.
d Eighteen and ten.
e Ivan. But everyone calls me Vanya.

Possessive nouns and adjectives

Possessive nouns

Add 's to a name or a noun.

Where is **Peter's** father from? What's the **teacher's** name?

Add an apostrophe (') to plural nouns that end in -s.

What are the **students'** names?

Add 's to the name or noun that comes last in a list of two or more.

When is **Sally and Hannah's** class?

Possessive adjectives

Where's Chad's father from? → Where's **his** father from?
What's Sheila's last name? → What's **her** last name?
What's Lee and Ping's address? → What's **their** address?

I → **my**
you → **your**
he → **his**
she → **her**
it → **its**
we → **our**
they → **their**

B Complete each sentence with a possessive form of the noun.

1 __________ (Dean) father is an engineer.
2 What is __________ (Janec) e-mail address?
3 The book is __________ (Kayla).
4 ____________________ (Nicole and Sean) class is at eight.
5 What are your __________ (brothers) occupations?

C On a separate sheet of paper, write a question for each answer, using What and a possessive adjective. Follow the example.

My occupation? I'm a student. *What's your occupation?*

1 Lin and Ben's? It's 2 Bay Street.
2 His phone number? It's 21-66-55.
3 Dave's last name? It's Bourne.
4 Sandra's nickname? It's Sandy.
5 My e-mail address? It's acme4@ymail.com.
6 Ray's? His address is 456 Rue Noire.

D Complete each sentence with a possessive adjective.

1 This is my sister. __________ husband is from Ecuador.
2 Robert is a new student here. __________ nickname is Bobby.
3 My friends live in London, but __________ hometown is in Scotland.
4 My husband and I live in Chicago, but __________ children don't.
5 I'd like you to meet __________ colleague Sam. He works with me at the bank.
6 I like that picture. __________ colors are very nice.

UNIT 1 *Lesson 2*

Verb be: usage and form

The verb be gives information about the subject of a sentence. The subject of a sentence can be a noun or a pronoun.

noun subject	pronoun subject
Our teacher is from the United States.	**She** is from the United States.
That school is new.	**It** is new.

Affirmative statements

There are three forms of the verb be in the present tense: am, is, and are.

I **am** a student. He / She / It } **is** late. You / We / They } **are** married.

Contracted forms

Contract be with subject nouns and pronouns. Use contractions in speaking and informal writing.

Robin is an artist. = **Robin's** an artist. I am a student. = **I'm** a student.
He is single. = **He's** single. You are on time. = **You're** on time.

Negative contractions

There are two ways to form negative contractions.

He**'s not** Brazilian. = He **isn't** Brazilian.
They**'re not** teachers. = They **aren't** teachers.

Note: There is only one way to contract I am not → I'm not.

Short answers with be: common errors

Don't use contractions with affirmative short answers to yes / no questions.

Are you a salesperson? Yes, I am. NOT ~~Yes, I'm.~~
Is he American? Yes, he is. NOT ~~Yes, he's.~~
Are they designers? Yes, they are. NOT ~~Yes, they're.~~

Note: It is also common to answer just with Yes or No.

Are you a salesperson? Yes.

A On a separate sheet of paper, write these sentences, using contractions. Then practice saying each sentence aloud.

1 She is an opera singer.
2 They are managers.
3 I am a student.
4 Bart is from Australia.
5 My mother is late.
6 Your father is nice.

B On a separate sheet of paper, write a short answer for each question.

1 Is New York in Russia?
2 Are you a scientist?
3 Are Korea and Japan in Asia?
4 Is Italy a city?
5 Is it 3:00 right now?
6 Are you a student?
7 Are you Canadian?
8 Is your father a manager?
9 Is English difficult?

Prepositions of time and place: usage rules

Time

Use on with the names of days or dates.

on Thursday	on Monday morning	on New Year's Day
on the weekend	on Sundays	on a weekday

Use in with periods of time (but not with names of days).

in 2008	in July	in [the] spring	in an hour
in the morning	in the 20th century	in the 1950s	in two weeks

Use at with specific moments in time.

at 9:00	at dawn	at noon
at sunrise	at dusk	at midnight

Place

Use on with the names of streets and specific physical locations.

on Main Street	on Smith Avenue	on the corner
on the street	on the right	on the left

Use in with the names of cities, countries, continents, and other large locations.

in the neighborhood	in the center of town	in Lima
in Korea	in Africa	in the ocean

Use at for buildings and addresses.

at the theater	at the supermarket	at the bank
at the train station	at 10 Main Street	

A Complete the following sentences with on, in, or at.

1 When's the movie? The movie is _____ Friday _____ 8:30.

2 _____ the weekend, I'm going to the concert _____ the public library.

3 Where is he? He's not here right now. He's _____ work.

4 Where's his office? It's _____ the center of town.

5 When was her mother born? She was born _____ January 1.

6 When does the movie take place? It takes place _____ the 19th century _____ Africa.

7 The park opens _____ 6:00 _____ the morning and closes _____ dusk.

8 Is the concert hall _____ Grove Street?

9 I think the theater is _____ the right side of the street.

10 Let's go to the evening show. The concert is outside, and the weather is really hot _____ the afternoon.

11 This concert occurs every second year _____ November.

12 I'll see you _____ Thursday morning in front of the theater, OK?

B Look at the tickets. On a separate sheet of paper, write questions with When or What time. Write a question with Where.

The simple present tense: usage and form

Usage

Use the simple present tense to talk about facts and habitual actions in the present.

facts	habitual actions
Josh **speaks** Spanish very well.	Josh **speaks** Spanish every day.
They **work** at Coffee Central.	They **work** late on Fridays.

Form

Add -s to the base form of the verb for third-person singular (he, she, or it).

I **like** Thai food.	He **likes** Peruvian food.
You **study** English.	She **studies** French.
They **open** at 6:00.	The store **opens** at 8:00.
We **work** at a café.	Marlene **works** at a school.

Negative forms

Use don't (do not) and doesn't (does not) + the base form of a verb to make negative statements.

I **don't like** American food. He **doesn't like** Greek food.

Yes / no questions

Use do or does + the base form of a verb to form yes / no questions.

Do you **speak** Portuguese? **Does** she **speak** French? NOT Does she ~~speaks~~ French?

A Write negative statements. Follow the example.

Gwen likes classical music. (Her sister) Her sister doesn't like classical music.

1 The café closes at 6:00. (The bookstore) ______

2 Neal lives in Quito. (His sister) ______

3 Miles works in an office. (His brother) ______

4 I have a big family. (My husband) ______

5 My younger brother speaks Chinese. (I) ______

6 Kiko's nephew likes hip-hop. (Her niece) ______

B Write yes / no questions. Follow the example.

A: Does your sister live near you? B: No, she doesn't. She lives in another city.

1 A: ______ drink coffee?
B: No, he doesn't. My brother drinks tea.

2 A: ______ children?
B: No, we don't have any yet.

3 A: ______ in Mexico?
B: No, my in-laws live in Chile.

4 A: ______ English?
B: Yes, she does. My niece speaks it well.

5 A: ______ work here?
B: Yes, they do. My cousins work downstairs.

6 A: ______ early?
B: No. The bookstore opens late.

Information questions in the simple present tense: form and common errors

Do and does

Use do or does + the base form of a verb to ask information questions.

Where **do** your in-laws **live**?
When **do** you **visit** your parents?
How often **do** they **go** to class?

Where **does** your sister **live**?
When **does** she **visit** her parents?
How often **does** he **go** to class?

Questions with who

Compare these questions with who.

	subject
Who visits your cousin in Chicago?	**My mother** does.

	object
Who does your mother visit in Chicago?	My mother visits **my cousin**.

Be careful! Don't use do or does with Who if the question is about the subject. Always use the third-person singular form to ask questions with Who about the subject.

Who **lives** here? NOT Who ~~does live~~ here? NOT Who ~~live~~ here?

How many

Be careful! Always use How many with plural nouns.

How many cousins do you have? NOT How many ~~cousin~~ do you have?

Complete the information questions.

1 ________________ your father __________? He's a doctor.
2 ________________ your in-laws __________? They live in Seoul.
3 ________________ cousins ________________? I have ten of them.
4 ______________________________ your parents? I visit them every weekend.
5 ________________ your sister __________? She lives across the street.
6 __________ speaks Russian? My brother-in-law does.
7 ________________ your aunt __________ with? She lives with my cousin.
8 ________________ you __________? I study late at night.
9 __________ has three kids? My sister does.
10 ________________ your older brother __________? He studies in London.

UNIT 4 ***Lesson 1***

Non-count nouns: categories and verb agreement

Non-count nouns are common in the following categories:

abstract ideas: health, advice, help, luck, fun
sports and activities: tennis, swimming, golf, basketball
illnesses: cancer, AIDS, diabetes, dengue
academic subjects: English, chemistry, art, mathematics
foods: rice, milk, sugar, coffee, fat

All non-count nouns require a singular verb.

Fat **isn't** good for you.
Mathematics **is** my favorite subject.

A Complete each sentence with the correct form of the verb.

1 Coffee __________ (be) my favorite beverage.

2 Rice __________ (be) very good for you, even when you are sick.

3 Mathematics __________ (create) problems for many students, but not for me!

4 Influenza __________ (cause) pain and fever.

5 Darkness ______________ (frighten) some people, but I don't know why.

6 Medical advice __________ (help) people decide what to do about their health.

B Complete the following sentences with a or an. If the noun is a non-count noun, write an X.

1 He has _____ diabetes.

2 She would like to eat _____ banana.

3 " _____ apple a day keeps the doctor away."

4 Would you like _____ appetizer?

5 There's _____ egg on the shelf.

6 Does the restaurant serve _____ rice with the chicken?

7 He always gives _____ good advice.

8 My family loves _____ music.

Non-count nouns: expressing quantities

We can make many non-count nouns countable:

a slice of bread, **a loaf of** bread, **three pieces of** bread, **two kinds of** bread

The following phrases are used with non-count nouns in order to make them countable:

liquids: a glass of, two cups of, a liter of, six gallons of, a bottle of, a can of

solids: a cup of, a piece of, three slices of, a kilo of, a spoonful of

C On a separate sheet of paper, complete each statement with a countable quantity. (Note: More than one phrase of quantity may be possible.)

liquids

1 This soup is so creamy. It has two ___ milk in it.

2 She must be very thirsty. This is her third ___ water.

3 My car has a big gas tank. It holds ___ gas.

solids

4 I ate ___ cheese and now I feel sick.

5 A club sandwich doesn't have two ___ bread. It has three ___ bread.

6 I like my tea sweet. Please put in ___ sugar.

Questions with How much and How many

Ask questions with How much for non-count nouns. Ask questions with How many for count nouns.

How much rice is in the soup?	Not much. Two cups.
How many eggs are in the fridge?	Not many. Three.

D Complete each question with How much or How many.

1 ______________ bread do we need?

2 ______________ salt did you put in the beef stew?

3 ______________ hot pepper do you like?

4 ______________ spoonfuls of sugar do you want in your tea?

5 ______________ oil should I put in this salad?

6 ______________ cheese is there in the fridge?

7 ______________ slices of bread do you want?

8 ______________ cups of coffee did you drink?

Words that can be count nouns or non-count nouns

Some nouns can be used as count or non-count nouns. The word is the same, but the meaning is different.

non-count use	count use
Chicken is delicious.	I bought two **chickens**.
Let's watch **TV**.	We have three **TVs** in our house.
The sun provides **light**.	It's too bright in here. Turn off one of the **lights**.

Some words can have a count sense or a non-count sense without any real difference in meaning.

I'm in the mood for **salad**. OR I'm in the mood for a **salad**.

I'd like **steak** for dinner. OR I'd like a **steak** for dinner.

Plural count nouns: spelling rules

Add -s to most nouns.

cup **cups** appetizer **appetizers** apple **apples**

If a noun ends in a consonant and -y, change the y to i and add -es.

cherry **cherries** berry **berries**

BUT: Do not change the y when the letter before the y is a vowel.

boy **boys**

Add -es to nouns that end in -ch, -o, -s, -sh, -x, or -z.

lunch **lunches** radish **radishes** tomato **tomatoes**
box **boxes** glass **glasses**

E Write the plural form of the following count nouns.

1 clam ______________
2 snack ______________
3 cup ______________
4 olive ______________
5 spoonful ______________
6 pear ______________
7 french fry ______________
8 sandwich ______________
9 vegetable ______________
10 potato ______________

UNIT 4 *Lesson 2*

Some and any

Use some and any to describe an indefinite number or amount.

There are **some** apples in the fridge. (Indefinite number: we don't know how many.)
Are there **any** oranges? (Indefinite number: no specific number being asked about.)
They are bringing us **some** coffee. (Indefinite amount: we don't know how much.)

Use some with non-count nouns and with plural count nouns in affirmative statements.

non-count noun — plural count noun
We need **some** milk and **some** bananas.

Use any with non-count nouns and plural count nouns in negative statements.

non-count noun — plural count noun
We don't want **any** cheese, and we don't need **any** apples.

Use any or some in questions with count and non-count nouns. There is no difference in meaning.

Do you need **any** cookies or butter? Do you need **some** cookies or butter?

A Change the following sentences from affirmative to negative. Follow the example.

There is some coffee in the kitchen. *There isn't any coffee in the kitchen.*
1 There are some onions on the table. ______________
2 We have some cookies. ______________
3 They need some onions for the soup. ______________
4 She's buying some fruit at the market. ______________
5 The Reeds want some eggs for breakfast. ______________
6 I want some butter on my sandwich. ______________
7 There is some chicken in the fridge. ______________
8 They need some cheese for the pasta. ______________

B Complete each sentence with some or any.

1 I don't want ________ more coffee, thank you.
2 There isn't ________ salt in this soup.
3 We don't see ________ sandwiches on the menu.
4 They need ________ sugar for their tea.
5 The restaurant is making ________ pies for the party.
6 It's too bad that there isn't ________ soup.
7 I don't see ________ menus on those tables.
8 There are ________ eggs for the omelette.

The present continuous: spelling rules for the present participle

The present continuous consists of two parts: a form of be and a present participle of a verb. To form a present participle, add -ing to the base form of a verb.

base form		present participle
talk	→	talking

If the base form ends in a silent (unvoiced) -e, drop the -e and add -ing.

leave	→	leaving

In verbs of one syllable, if the last three letters are a consonant-vowel-consonant* sequence, double the last consonant and then add -ing to the base form.

C V C
s i t → sitting

BUT: If the base form of the verb ends in -w, -x, or -y, don't double the final consonant.

blow	→	**blowing**
fix	→	**fixing**
say	→	**saying**

If a base form has more than one syllable and ends in a consonant-vowel-consonant sequence, double the last consonant only if the spoken stress is on the last syllable.

per - mit → permitting BUT or - der → ordering

* **Vowels** = a, e, i, o, u
* **Consonants** = b, c, d, f, g, h, j, k, l, m, n, p, q, r, s, t, v, w, x, y, z

A Write the present participle for each of the following base forms. Follow the rules.

1 turn ______	7 stop ______	13 sew ______	19 change ______
2 rain ______	8 exit ______	14 listen ______	20 be ______
3 run ______	9 sit ______	15 do ______	21 have ______
4 help ______	10 eat ______	16 write ______	22 put ______
5 open ______	11 buy ______	17 begin ______	23 go ______
6 close ______	12 mix ______	18 use ______	24 pay ______

The present continuous: rules for forming statements

Remember to form the present continuous with be and a present participle of a verb.

affirmative statements	**negative statements**
I'm **studying** English.	I'm not **studying** French.
You're **studying** French.	You're not **studying** English.
He's **reading** a book.	He's not **reading** a newspaper.
She's **reading** a newspaper.	She's not **reading** a book.
We're **watching** TV.	We're not **watching** a DVD.
They're **watching** a video.	They're not **watching** TV.

B On a separate sheet of paper, change each affirmative statement to a negative statement. Use contractions.

1 She's going to the supermarket.
2 He's calling his wife this afternoon.
3 I'm cooking dinner tonight.
4 The Roberts are feeding their kids early.
5 Joel's taking the bus to the movies.
6 We're getting a new printer.

C Write answers to the following questions in complete affirmative or negative statements. Use the present continuous and contractions.

1 Are you studying English this weekend? ______________________________

2 When are you taking a vacation? ______________________________

3 Is it raining now? ______________________________

4 Where are you eating dinner tonight? ______________________________

5 Are you listening to music now? ______________________________

6 Who's making breakfast tomorrow? ______________________________

The present continuous: rules for forming questions

Yes / no questions: Place a form of be before the subject of the sentence. (Invert the subject and verb be.)

Is she watching TV?
Are you driving there?
Is Stu shopping?
Are we meeting this afternoon?
Are they talking on the phone?
Are Nan and Bert studying?

Information questions: Use question words to ask information questions. (Invert the subject and verb be.)

When are you going?
What are you doing right now?
Who is he watching on TV?
How much are you paying for that computer?
Why are you buying that laptop?

Be careful with Who when asking a question about the subject:

Who's talking on the phone? (John is.)

D Write a question in the present continuous to complete each conversation.

1. A: ______________________________?
B: No. Luke's not watching TV right now.

2 A: ______________________________?
B: Yes, She's working this morning.

3 A: ______________________________?
B: I'm calling Janet Hammond.

4 A: ______________________________?
B: She's coming home later tonight.

TOP NOTCH
1A
Writing Booster

Writing Booster

The Writing Booster is optional. It is intended to teach students the conventions of written English. Each unit's Writing Booster is focused both on a skill and its application to the Writing Exercise from the Unit Review page.

UNIT 1 *Capitalization*

Use a capital letter to begin a sentence.
It's a pleasure to introduce my classmate.

Use a capital letter for:

cities / countries	I live in **B**eijing. He's from **C**olombia.
nationalities	They're **H**onduran.
languages	I speak **R**ussian and **I**talian.
days and months	My birthday is on **T**uesday, **J**une 19th.
with the word I	My brother and **I** are students.
formal titles and names	I'd like you to meet **M**r. **S**mith.

A On a separate sheet of paper, rewrite each sentence, using correct capitalization.

1 please say hello to julio cueva from peru.
2 my friend mr. lee is a computer programmer from korea.
3 he is brazilian, and his birthday is in october.
4 my classmate ms. silva is twenty-six years old.
5 miss wang teaches chinese to college students.
6 this monday john met his friend mr. abe.
7 when i travel, i need to use english.

B Guidance for Writing (page 12) **Ask a classmate the questions below. Use the answers as a guide for your writing. Add more information if you can. Make sure you use capital letters correctly.**

- What's your partner's name?
- Does your partner have a nickname?
- How old is your partner?
- What's your partner's occupation?
- What is your partner's hometown?
- Is your partner's hometown his or her birthplace?
- What's your partner's favorite actor?
- What's your partner's favorite sport?

UNIT 2 *The sentence*

In English, a sentence is a group of words that expresses a thought. A sentence has a subject and a verb. When you write a sentence, begin with a capital letter and end with a period.

subject	verb	subject	verb
The play	is great.	She	loves music.

A Circle the subject and underline the verb in each sentence.

1 Her children like folk music.
2 I prefer CDs to cassettes.
3 My boyfriend loves classical music.
4 Their favorite musician is Beck.
5 The play isn't very good.

B Write an X next to the words or groups of words that are not sentences.

☐ 1 A theater fan.
☐ 2 The theater is down the street from the park.
☐ 3 And around the corner from the art gallery.
☐ 4 I listen to music in the shower.
☐ 5 Really loud concerts.
☐ 6 Downloading music.

C Guidance for Writing (page 24) **Use the ideas as a guide to help you write five sentences about your musical tastes. Begin each sentence with a capital letter and end each sentence with a period. Be sure to use a subject and a verb in each sentence.**

Ideas
- your favorite music
- your favorite artist
- when you listen to music
- where you buy music
- how many CDs you own

UNIT 3 *Combining sentences with and or but*

And

Use and to combine two sentences if you want to add information. It's common, but not necessary, to use a comma before and.

My cousin loves rock music, **and** she's a great dancer.

But

Use but to combine two sentences if you want to show a difference or contrast. It's common, but not necessary, to use a comma before but.

My cousin loves rock music, **but** I love classical.
My cousin loves rock music, **but** I don't.

Be careful! In traditional formal writing, writers avoid beginning sentences with And or But.

Don't write: My cousin loves rock music. ~~And she's a great dancer.~~
Don't write: My cousin loves rock music. ~~But I don't.~~

A On a separate sheet of paper, combine these sentences, using and.

1 My sister-in-law has long hair. She's very pretty.
2 My aunt is a computer programmer. Her husband is a teacher.
3 We look alike. We wear the same clothes.
4 My cousin likes classical music. He loves Italian food.
5 We look completely different. We like different kinds of music.

B On a separate sheet of paper, combine these sentences, using but.

1 My brother wears old clothes. I wear new clothes.
2 My sister has long hair. I have short hair.
3 My cousin lives near the airport. His parents don't.
4 I love rock music. My stepfather doesn't.
5 We look alike. We wear completely different clothes.

C Guidance for Writing (page 36) **Use the ideas to help you write six statements comparing two people in your family. Use and or but to combine sentences.**

Ideas
- appearance
- musical tastes
- food preferences
- clothing preferences
- birthplaces and hometowns
- marital status
- favorite colors

UNIT 4 *Connecting words and ideas with and or in addition*

And

Remember that and connects two sentences and makes them one sentence.

I like fruit, **and** I also like vegetables.

You can also use and to connect words in a series. Notice the use of the comma in the examples below.

I like apples, oranges, grapes, **and** other fruits.

Be careful! Don't use a comma when and connects only two words.

I like apples and oranges. NOT ~~I like apples, and oranges~~.

In addition

In addition connects the ideas in one sentence with the ideas in the next sentence. Use a comma after in addition.

I like fruit. **In addition,** I like vegetables.
I like apples and oranges. **In addition,** I like grapes and other fruits.

A Connect the following words and ideas with and or in addition.

1 The people eat a lot of vegetables in Spain, Italy, ________________ France.
2 In the U.S., many restaurants serve big portions. ________________ , there are a lot of fatty foods.
3 There are five or six great Italian restaurants near the hotel. ________________ , there are two restaurants where the menu has dishes from Mexico, Thailand, India, ________________ even Indonesia!
4 She loves pasta, ________________ I want to invite her to my favorite Italian restaurant.
5 Raw carrots taste great, ________________ they're good for you.
6 This restaurant has great food. ________________ , the service is excellent.
7 You can choose from six entrées on the menu, ________________ they all come with a choice of vegetable.
8 I usually order soup, salad, a main course, ________________ dessert.

B Guidance for Writing (page 48) Read the description of food in the United States. Use these paragraphs as a guide to help you write about the food of your country. Change the details so the sentences describe your food.

American food is more than hamburgers, hot dogs, and pancakes. The best American food is regional. One regional specialty is clam chowder. Clam chowder is a delicious soup from the northeast coast. In Boston, clam chowder contains milk, and in New York it contains tomatoes. Clam chowder always contains Atlantic clams. In addition, clam chowder always contains some vegetables, such as onions, potatoes, peppers, or corn.

Another famous regional specialty of American cooking is barbecue. Barbecue comes from the center and south of the United States. Barbecue style is not always the same, but it always has meat and a spicy sauce. Americans are very proud of barbecue. Many restaurants claim that they have the only authentic barbecue. When you travel to the United States, be sure to try some regional specialties like clam chowder and barbecue.

UNIT 5 *Placement of adjectives: before nouns and after the verb be*

Adjectives are words that describe nouns and pronouns.

The old **photocopier** (noun) is obsolete. **It**'s (pronoun) also broken.

Adjectives come before nouns or after the verb be when the subject of a sentence is a noun or pronoun.

I have a **new computer**.
The computer **is new**. It**'s terrific**.

Be careful! Adjectives don't come after nouns. Adjectives don't have plural forms.

new refrigerators
NOT ~~refrigerators new~~
NOT ~~news~~ refrigerators

When two adjectives describe the same noun, connect them with and. When there are more than two, use commas.

The microwave is **popular** and **convenient**.
This camera is **obsolete**, **broken**, and **defective**.

Adjectives

broken	fast
obsolete	popular
defective	guaranteed
terrible	affordable
awful	convenient
great	good
terrific	fixable
awesome	

Some adjectives are compound phrases.

This scanner is really **up-to-date**.
She bought an **out-of-date** camcorder.

A Circle the adjectives in each sentence.

1 My old printer is obsolete.
2 This MP3 is very convenient. And it's portable, too.
3 Is your scanner fixable?
4 This terrible car is a lemon! It's awful.
5 Our new washing machine is both good and guaranteed.

B On a separate sheet of paper, write sentences about five of the following products. Use the adjectives from the chart above.

Products

a smart phone	a digital camera
a mobile / cell phone	a TV
a GPS	a camcorder
a laptop (computer)	A DVD player
a desktop (computer)	

Smart phones are very convenient.

C Guidance for Writing (page 60) Use your answers to the following questions as a guide to help you write a paragraph about a product you use.

- What is it?
- What brand is it?
- What model is it?
- Is it a good product? Why or why not?
- What does it do?
- What adjectives describe it?
- Where do you use it?
- Is it working?
- Does it drive you crazy?
- How old is it?

Top Notch Pop Lyrics

1:15/1:16

It's Nice To Meet You [Unit 1]

(CHORUS)

It's nice to meet you.
Good to meet you.
Pleasure to meet you.

What's your name?
My name is Mr. Johnson.
Please just call me Stan.
I'd like you to meet my wife, Mary Anne.

(CHORUS)

What do you do?
Actually, I'm a teacher
at the Children's Institute.
The little kids are really cute.
That sounds nice. Where are you from—
somewhere far or near?
As a matter of fact, Chicago is my
hometown.
Could you say that louder please?
How did you end up here?
My father was a salesman.
We moved all around.

(CHORUS)

Who is that?
Let me introduce you
to my new friend Eileen.
She's a chef and she's nineteen.

(CHORUS)

Good-bye. Take care.

1:34/1:35

Going Out [Unit 2]

Do you want to see a play?
What time does the play begin?
It starts at eight. Is that OK?
I'd love to go. I'll see you then.
I heard it got some good reviews.
Where's it playing? What's the show?
It's called "One Single Life to Lose."
I'll think about it. I don't know.

(CHORUS)

Everything will be all right
when you and I go out tonight.

When Thomas Soben gives his talk—
The famous chef? That's not for me!
The doors open at nine o'clock.
There's a movie we could see
at Smith and Second Avenue.
That's my favorite neighborhood!
I can't wait to be with you.
I can't wait to have some food.

(CHORUS)

We're going to have a good time.
Don't keep me up past my bedtime.
We'll make a date.
Tonight's the night.
It starts at eight.
The price is right!
I'm a fan of rock 'n' roll.
Classical is more my style.
I like blues and I like soul.
Bach and Mozart make me smile!
Around the corner and down the street.
That's the entrance to the park.
There's a place where we could meet.
I wouldn't go there after dark!

(CHORUS: 2 times)

2:18/2:19

An Only Child [Unit 3]

Let me see the photos of
your wife and family.
Who's that guy there, on the right,
next to the TV?
Is that your younger brother, John?
And who are those two?
Your sisters both look so alike.
Please tell me what they do.

(CHORUS)

I ask so many questions.
You just answer with a smile.
You have a large family,
but I am an only child.

How about your cousins now?
Please tell me something new.
Do they both play basketball?
You know that I do, too.

(CHORUS)

I don't have a brother,
but you have two or three.
You're all one big happy family.
I don't have a sister,
but you have older twins.
This is a game I can't ever win.
Do you have nieces and nephews,
and how many are there now?
Do they all like the same kinds of things?
Are they different somehow?

(CHORUS)

2:34/2:35

The World Café [Unit 4]

Is there something that you want?
Is there anything you need?
Have you made up your mind
what you want to eat?
Place your order now,
or do you need more time?
Why not start with some juice—
lemon, orange, or lime?
Some like it hot, some like it sweet,
some like it really spicy.
You may not like everything you eat,
but I think we're doing nicely.

(CHORUS)

I can understand every word you say.
Tonight we're speaking English at
The World Café.

I'll take the main course now.
I think I'll have the fish.
Does it come with the choice of another
dish?
Excuse me waiter, please—
I think I'm in the mood
for a little dessert, and the cake looks good.
Do you know? Are there any low-fat desserts
that we could try now?
I feel like having a bowl of fruit.
Do you have to say good-bye now?

(CHORUS)

Apples, oranges, cheese, and ham,
coffee, juice, milk, bread, and jam,
rice and beans, meat and potatoes,
eggs and ice cream,
grilled tomatoes—
That's the menu.
That's the list.
Is there anything I missed?

(CHORUS)

3:22/3:23

It's Not Working Again [Unit 5]

Hi. I'm calling on my cell phone.
I need a little help with a fax machine.
It's not working, and it's pretty bad.
I feel like I've been had, if you know
what I mean.
I'm coming to the store right now.
Can you show me how to use it?
The front lid won't open.
When my cat's around,
it squeaks and makes a funny sound.

(CHORUS)

It's not working again.
It's driving me crazy.
It's not working again.

I called yesterday, and a guy named Jack
said,
"I'm busy right now, can I call you back?"
He didn't even ask me what was wrong
with it.
He didn't want to hear the short and
long of it.
I just bought the thing yesterday,
and it won't turn on so please don't say,
"I'm sorry to hear that.
That's a shame.
That's too bad."
It's all a game.

(CHORUS)

I'm not looking for a laptop computer
or an X340 or a PDA.
Just tell me what's wrong with my fax
machine
so I can say good-bye and be on my way.
It won't send a copy of my document.
The paper goes through, and it comes
out bent.
On second thought, it's guaranteed.
I want my money back—that's what I need.

(CHORUS: 2 times)

3:40/3:41

A Typical Day [Unit 6]

The Couch Potato sits around.
He eats junk food by the pound.
It's just a typical day.
Watching as the world goes by,
he's out of shape and wonders why.
It's just a typical day.

(CHORUS)

Every night he dreams that he's
skydiving through the air.
And sometimes you appear.
He says, "What are you doing here?"

He cleans the house and plays guitar,
takes a shower, drives the car.
It's just a typical day.
He watches TV all alone,
reads and sleeps, talks on the phone.
It's just a typical day.

(CHORUS)

I'm sorry.
Mr. Couch Potato's resting right now.
Can he call you back?
He usually lies down every day of the week,
and he always has to have a snack.
Now all his dreams are coming true.
He's making plans to be with you.
It's just a typical day.
He goes dancing once a week.
He's at the theater as we speak!
It's just a typical day.

(CHORUS)

4:17/4:18

My Dream Vacation [Unit 7]

The ride was bumpy
and much too long.
It was pretty boring.
It felt so wrong.
I slept all night,
and it rained all day.
We left the road,
and we lost the way.
Then you came along
and you took my hand.
You whispered words
I could understand.

(CHORUS)

On my dream vacation,
I dream of you.
I don't ever want to wake up.
On my dream vacation,
this much is true:
I don't ever want it to stop.

The food was awful.
They stole my purse.
The whole two weeks went
from bad to worse.
They canceled my ticket.
I missed my flight.
They were so unfriendly
it just wasn't right.
So I called a taxi,
and I got inside,
and there you were,
sitting by my side.

(CHORUS)

You were so unusual.
The day was so exciting.
I opened up my eyes,
and you were gone.
I waited for hours.
You never called.
I watched TV
and looked at the walls.
Where did you go to?
Why weren't you near?
Did you have a reason
to disappear?
So I flew a plane
to the south of France,
and I heard you say,
Would you like to dance?"

(CHORUS)

4:35/4:36

Anything Goes [Unit 8]

The shoe department's upstairs.
It's on the second floor.
Women's Casual is down the stairs,
there by the door.
This helpful store directory
shows every kind of clothes.
I look for the department where
it says anything goes.

(CHORUS)

At home and when I travel,
I always like to wear
pajamas in the daytime
with a blazer and a pair
of socks on my fingers
and gloves on my toes—
anything goes.

On the ground floor, there's a restaurant
and a photo studio,
so I take the escalator
down to the floor below.
There are turtlenecks and T-shirts.
There are cardigans and jeans
in every size and color.
They look comfortable and clean.

(CHORUS)

The salesperson says,
"Here you go.
Try it on.
That's not too bad.
Let me see if I can find you something
better."
Some people say that black clothes
are more flattering than white,
or they think that they look nicer
in the day or in the night.
Their clothes can't be too liberal
or too conservative.
If I love it, then I wear it.
That's the way I want to live.

(CHORUS)

5:18/5:19

Five Hundred Ways [Unit 9]

You could take the bus,
or you could take the train.
You could take the ferry,
or you could take a plane.
Baby, it's a small world,
when all is said and done.
We have so many options,
the question is, which one?

(CHORUS)

There are five hundred ways to get here.
What are you going to do?
You could get a one-way ticket to see me.
I'm waiting here for you.

You should really hurry.
When are you going to call
and make your reservation?
You could miss them all.
And do you know how long
you are going to stay?
You could come and be with me
forever and a day.

(CHORUS)

Follow me.
Follow me.
Yes, you can follow me.
You have my phone number,
and you have my address.
Tell me, are you coming on
the local or express?

(CHORUS)

5:34/5:35

Shopping for Souvenirs [Unit 10]

I go to the bank at a quarter to ten.
I pick up my cash from the ATM.
Here at the store, it won't be too hard
to take out a check or a credit card.
The bank has a good rate of exchange,
and everything here is in my price range.
The easiest part of this bargain hunt
is that I can afford anything I want.

(CHORUS)

Whenever I travel around the world,
I spend my money for two.
Shopping for souvenirs
helps me to be near you.

I try to decide how much I should pay
for the beautiful art I see on display.
To get a great deal, I can't be too nice.
It can't hurt to ask for a better price.

(CHORUS)

Yes, it's gorgeous, and I love it.
It's the biggest and the best,
though it might not be the cheapest.
How much is it—more than all the rest?
I'll pass on some good advice to you:
When you're in Rome, do as the Romans do.
A ten percent tip for the taxi fare
should be good enough when you're staying
there.

(CHORUS)

SECOND EDITION

TOP NOTCH 1A

Workbook

Joan Saslow • Allen Ascher

With Barbara R. Denman and Julie C. Rouse

UNIT 1

Getting Acquainted

Preview

1 **Read about the famous person. Then check <u>true</u>, <u>false</u>, or <u>no information</u>, according to the website.**

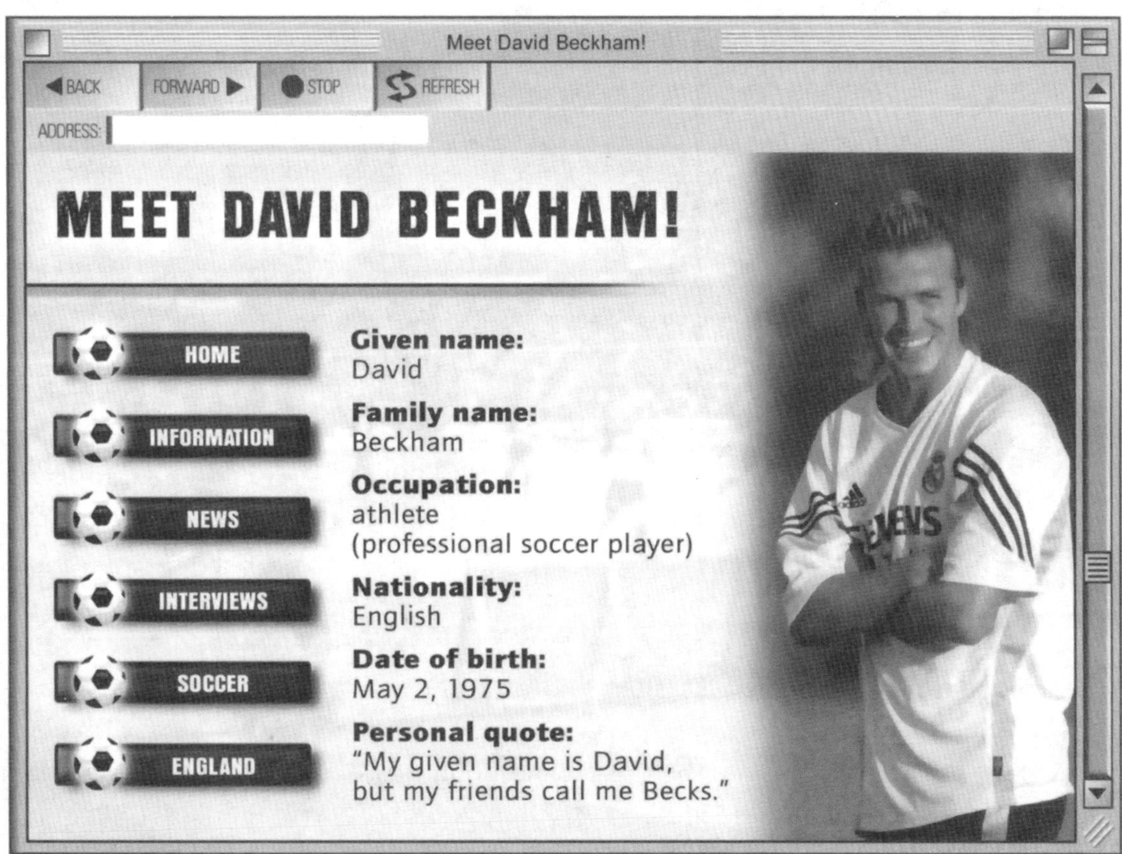

Source: www.beckham-magazine.com

	true	false	no information
1. His first name is David.	☑	☐	☐
2. His last name is Becks.	☐	☑	☐
3. He is an actor.	☐	☑	☐
4. He is married.	☐	☐	☑
5. His nickname is David.	☐	☐	☑

2 **Match the word or words with the same meaning. Draw a line.**

1. Nice to meet you.
2. first name
3. last name
4. single

a. not married
b. given name
c. It's a pleasure to meet you.
d. family name

3 **Introduce David Beckham. Complete the quote. Use a formal title.**

"I'd like to introduce you to ____

____."

4 **Complete the information. Write your name on the lines.**

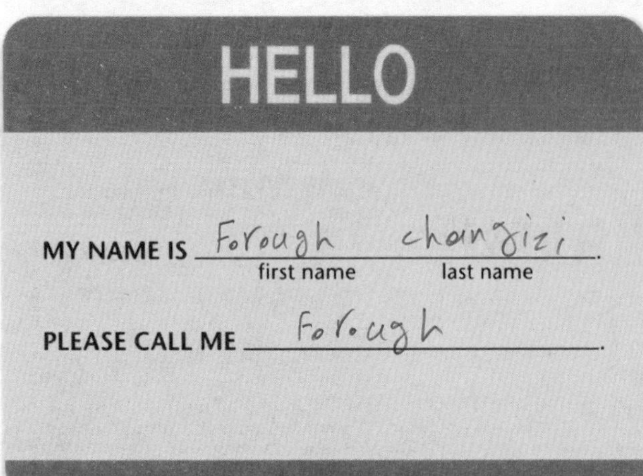

LESSON 1

5 **Choose the correct response. Circle the letter.**

1. "Who's that?"
   a. Please call me Matt. b. Great to meet you. c. That's my brother, Ryan.
2. "My name's Sidney, and this is Sam."
   a. Hi. I'm Rachel. b. I think they're new. c. I'm from Australia.
3. "My name's Elizabeth, but everyone calls me Ellie."
   a. Let's say hello. b. It's a pleasure to meet you. c. I'd like you to meet Ellie.
4. "Where are you from?"
   a. London. b. Twenty-five. c. A student.

6 **Complete the information questions. Use contractions when possible.**

1. A: who's that?
   B: That's Mr. Miller.
2. A: what's her occupation?
   B: She's an artist.
3. A: Your son is very cute. How old is he?
   B: He's eight months old.
4. A: I'll send you an e-mail. what's your e-mail address?
   B: It's une-yoshiko@videotech.co.jp.
5. A: where are Anil and Temel from?
   B: They're from Istanbul, I think.
6. A: ________________ your new classmates?
   B: That's Marcos on the right and Paulo on the left.

7 Choose the correct response. Write the letter on the line.

c 1. "How old is Michael?"
d 2. "Who's not here?"
F 3. "What are your occupations?"
b 4. "Where are their friends from?"
a 5. "Where is Ava?"
g 6. "What city is he from"
e 7. "Who are your teachers?"

a. She's over there.
b. They're from Germany.
c. He's three.
d. Rachel isn't here.
e. Their names are Mr. Park and Ms. Kim.
f. I'm a singer, and he's a student.
g. He's from Tokyo.

8 Look at the picture. Write a question for each answer.

1. A: ______________________________?
   B: They're my friends from computer class.
2. A: ______________________________?
   B: Their names are Juan and Paloma.
3. A: ______________________________?
   B: Spain.
4. A: ______________________________?
   B: She's two years old.

9 Answer the questions. Use your own words.

1. "Who's your teacher?"
   YOU ______________________________
2. "What's your e-mail address?"
   YOU ______________________________
3. "How old are you?"
   YOU ______________________________

LESSON 2

10 Unscramble the words to write sentences.

1. actor / wonderful / is / Dev Patel / a
   ____
2. fantastic / a / athlete / is / Lance Armstrong
   ____
3. Gabriel Garcia Márquez / writer / is / great / a
   ____
4. are / musicians / The Gipsy Kings / excellent
   ____
5. beautiful / is / Zhang Ziyi / and actress / a / singer
   ____
6. chef / a / Nobu Matsuhisa / famous / is
   ____

11 Look at the responses. Complete the yes / no questions with be.

1. A: Are y.u Stacey?
   B: No, I'm not. I'm Claire.
2. A: Are they English?
   B: No, they're not. They're Australian.
3. A: __________ a student here?
   B: Yes, he is. I think he's new.
4. A: Are y.a married?
   B: No, I'm not. I'm single.
5. A: __________ in the same class?
   B: Yes, we are.
6. A: __________ a good chef?
   B: She sure is.

12 Look at the picture. Write short answers about the people.

Andy and Tara

1. Are Andy and Tara students?
   Yes, they are.

John

2. Is John an athlete?
   Yes he is

Maria

3. Is Maria from Venezuela?
   No she isnt

Linda and Mike

4. Are Linda and Mike married?
   yes they are

13 CHALLENGE. Write yes / no questions with be about the people from Exercise 10.

1. Dev Patel / from the movie *Slumdog Millionaire* ______
2. Lance Armstrong / a soccer player ______
3. Mr. Garcia Márquez / a Nobel Prize winner ______
4. The Gipsy Kings' songs / in French ______
5. Zhang Ziyi / from Hong Kong ______
6. Nobu Matsuhisa / sushi chef ______

Can you answer the questions? Write short answers. Use contractions when possible. If you don't know, guess.

1. Yes, he is.
2. ______
3. ______
4. ______
5. ______
6. ______

14 Answer the questions. Use your own words.

1. "Are you a good singer?" YOU No I'm not
2. "Are you a good athlete?" YOU No I'm not
3. "Are any of your friends or family members famous?" YOU ______

LESSONS 3 and 4

15 Read about where the people are from. Guess their nationalities. Use yes / no questions.

1. A: "My hometown is Vancouver."
   B: ______?
2. A: "I'm from Beijing."
   B: ______?
3. A: "I'm originally from London."
   B: ______?
4. A: "I'm actually from Istanbul."
   B: ______?

16 Answer the questions. Use your own words.

1. "What's your nationality?" YOU ______
2. "What's your birthplace?" YOU ______
3. "What's your hometown?" YOU ______
4. "What's your occupation?" YOU ______
5. "What's your nickname?" YOU ______

17 **Read the letter and reply on an intercultural exchange website.**

Ask Allen — Advice for International Travelers

Favorites | History | Search

What's in a first name? In many countries, it's the last.

Dear Allen,

I have a problem. My name is Chinese. It's Zhang Yin. Zhang is my last name and Yin is my first name. In China, family names are first and given names are last. I'm a salesman and I often travel to English-speaking countries for business. When I fill out a personal information form in English, I write Yin in the box for first name and Zhang in the box for last name. Then people call me Yin Zhang. When I introduce myself as Zhang Yin, they call me Mr. Yin. So sometimes I say that my name is Yin Zhang. But I don't feel comfortable with that because that isn't my real name. What should I do?

Zhang Yin

Shanghai, China

Dear Yin,

In English-speaking countries, when you ask, "What's your name?" you always get the person's given name first and the family name last. In China, and in many Asian countries, including Japan and Korea, the family name is first and given name is second. To avoid confusion, try introducing yourself like this: "Hi. I'm Zhang Yin. My first name is Yin and my family name is Zhang. Please call me Mr. Zhang."

Allen

Now read the sentences. Check true, false, or no information.

	true	false	no information
1. Zhang Yin's nationality is Chinese.	☐	☐	☐
2. Zhang Yin's family name is Yin.	☐	☐	☐
3. Zhang Yin is a computer programmer.	☐	☐	☐
4. Zhang Yin is married.	☐	☐	☐
5. In China, you say a person's family name first.	☐	☐	☐

Read the article "Who Uses English?" on page 10 of the Student's Book again. Answer the questions.

1. What is the nationality of Ms. Marques's company?

____

2. How does Ms. Marques use English in her free time?

____

3. Who is Mr. Yuan's wife? What is her occupation?

____

4. How does Mr. Yuan use English at home?

____

5. Who is Mr. Stolze's wife? What is her occupation?

____

6. How do you use English in your free time?

____

19 **Read about a famous athlete.**

Roger Federer

Name:	Roger Federer
Nickname:	Federer Express
Occupation:	Professional athlete (tennis player)
Date of birth:	August 8, 1981
Nationality:	Swiss
Hometown:	Basel, Switzerland
Now lives in:	Wollerau, Switzerland

Interesting facts: He speaks Swiss-German, English, German, and French (also some Swedish and Italian). He is the father of twin girls, Charlene Riva and Myla Rose, born in 2009. In his free time, he likes to play videogames.

Source: wikipedia.org

Now write a paragraph introducing Roger Federer. Use the paragraphs on page 11 of the Student's Book as a model.

GRAMMAR BOOSTER

A Look at the responses. Write information questions. Use contractions when possible.

1. A: *What's your name?*
   B: It's Margaret. But my nickname is Maggie.
2. A: ______________________
   B: My son? He's five.
3. A: ______________________
   B: I'm from Ukraine.
4. A: ______________________
   B: They are my brothers. Their names are Ishaan and Mahin.
5. A: ______________________
   B: It's agarcia@ecotech.com. I check my work e-mail every day.

B Add apostrophes (') to the possessive nouns.

1. My <u>parents</u> nationalities? My mom is Korean, and my dad is Irish.
2. Our <u>teachers</u> name is Mr. Springer.
3. <u>Rosas</u> hometown is Recife, in Brazil.
4. The <u>salespersons</u> wife is from Canada. Her English is excellent.
5. Adriana has two boys and a girl. Her <u>sons</u> birthplace is Quito, but her <u>daughters</u> birthplace is New York.

C Complete each sentence with a possessive adjective from the box.

my	your	his	her	our	their

1. Anya and Simon are new students. ________ teacher is Mr. Michaels.
2. Mr. Vidal is a computer programmer. ________ family lives in Paris.
3. Mrs. Ichikawa is from Tokyo. ________ nationality is Japanese.
4. Are you a photographer? ________ pictures are fantastic.
5. I'd like you to meet ________ sister Sarah. She's a musician.
6. Lucy and I are in a computer class. ________ class is at 9 A.M.

D Complete the conversations with words from the box.

they	their	you	your	he	his	she	her	we	our

1. A: Who's that?
   B: That's Ajit's brother. ________ name is Raj.
   A: How old is ________?
   B: Twenty-three, I think.
2. A: Are ________ the new English teacher?
   B: Yes, I am.
   A: Hi, I'm Chung. What's ________ name?
   B: David Lane. But everyone calls me DJ.
3. A: These are my two sons.
   B: What are ________ names?
   A: Jack and Owen.
   B: Are ________ students?
   A: yes, they are.
4. A: Hi, Ha-na.
   B: Hello, Su-ji. Are ________ classmates again?
   A: Yes, I think so. Is that ________ teacher over there?
   B: Yes. ________ name is Mrs. Kim.
   A: ________ looks very young!

E **Complete the sentences. Use contractions.**

1. You don't know where Liverpool is? ____________ in England.
2. My job is wonderful. ____________ an interpreter, and I meet people from all over the world.
3. Ms. Kusefoglu's hometown is Konya. ____________ Turkish.
4. His name is Mr. Yu. ____________ a photographer.
5. Our children are James and Lily. ____________ six and four years old.
6. Irina and I are from Ukraine. ____________ Russian.
7. She lives in São Paulo, but ____________ Brazilian. She's from Argentina.
8. Chang is his family name. ____________ his given name.

F **Answer the yes / no questions with short answers. Answer the information questions with complete sentences. Use contractions when possible.**

1. Is David Beckham American? ____________________
2. What is his occupation? ____________________
3. Is Mr. Beckham's nickname Becks? ____________________
4. Are you a fan of soccer? ____________________
5. Where is Roger Federer from? ____________________
6. Is Mr. Federer married? ____________________
7. Are you a tennis player? ____________________
8. How old are Mr. Beckham and Mr. Federer? ____________________

WRITING BOOSTER

A **Look at the personal information. Correct the capitalization.**

G

Name: geraldo rivera rodriguez

Nickname: jerry

Date of birth: july 31, 1973

Occupation: singer

Hometown: levittown, puerto rico (near san juan)

Birthplace: humacao, puerto rico

Favorite music: salsa

Favorite singer: frankie ruiz

B **Rewrite the following paragraph. Use correct capitalization.**

naomi watts is a famous actress. her date of birth is september 28, 1968.
ms. watts's hometown is sydney, australia, but her birthplace is shoreham, kent, england.
now she lives in los angeles. the actress says, "i feel british, australian, and american."
she can speak english with three different accents. this is great for her occupation.
ms. watts has two sons, alexander and samuel. their nicknames are sacha and sammy.

C **Write a short description of Jerry Rivera. Use the information from Exercise A. Use the paragraph from Exercise B as a guide.**

UNIT 2

Going Out

Preview

1 **Look at the newspaper concert listings. Then complete the chart.**

An evening of classical music with world-renowned classical pianist

Alfred Brendel

Beethoven's piano sonatas Nos. 8, 9, and 13.
Performance begins at 8:00 P. M. at City Music Hall.
Tickets are $45.

Who is playing?	What kind of music?	Where is it?	What time is the show?	How much are tickets?
Marc Anthony	Latin		10:30 P.M.	
James Carter		Riverfront Park		
				$15
	classical	City Music Hall		

2 **What's your style? Check <u>Not for me</u> or <u>More my style</u>.**

Kind of concert	Not for me	More my style
an afternoon jazz concert in the park	☐	☐
a late night rock concert at a club	☐	☐
a classical concert at a concert hall	☐	☐
live salsa music at a dance club	☐	☐

3 **Complete the paragraph with kinds of music and concert times. Use your own words.**

I like ____________ music, but ____________ music isn't really my style. A concert at ____________ is too late, but a concert at ____________ is perfect for me.

LESSON 1

4 Choose the correct response. Circle the letter.

1. "What time's the show?"
   a. At the theater. b. On Thursday. c. At 8:30.
2. "I'm busy on Friday. Maybe some other time."
   a. How about Friday? b. Perfect! c. Too bad.
3. "Where's the concert?"
   a. In the park. b. In ten minutes. c. On August 2nd.
4. "Are you free on Sunday at noon? There's a great exhibit at Gallery Z."
   a. I'd love to go. b. That's past my bedtime. c. What time?

5 Put the conversation in order. Write the number on the line.

__1__ Are you busy on Saturday night?

____ 10:00 P.M.? Well, I'd like to go, but that's past my bedtime.

____ Really? Sounds great! What time's the play?

____ *Mamma Mia!* is at the Community Theater.

____ At 10:00 P.M. It's a late show.

____ No, I'm not. Why?

____ Too bad. Maybe some other time.

6 Complete the sentences with on, in, or at.

1. The movie theater is ____ Dewey Street.
2. The play is ____ noon, ____ the park.
3. Ana isn't here. She's ____ New York.
4. Her class is ____ the Newtown Music School. It's ____ the corner of 2nd and Park.
5. The talk is ____ 11:00 ____ the morning.
6. The Shakira concert is ____ Friday, January 18th.
7. I can't talk right now. I'm ____ work. I'll call you when I get home.
8. Great! I'll meet you in front of the theater ____ twenty minutes.

7 Write questions with When, Where, or What time. Use contractions when possible.

1. A: When's the play? B: The play is on Wednesday.
2. A: ____________________? B: The concert is at 7:00.
3. A: ____________________? B: The school is on Saddle Avenue.
4. A: ____________________? B: Michael's at work.
5. A: ____________________? B: My class is on Monday morning.
6. A: ____________________? B: The exhibit is at the Art Center.
7. A: ____________________? B: The author's talk is at 7:30.

8 Answer the questions. Use your own words. Use in, on, or at.

1. "Where is your school?"

   YOU ______________________________

2. "What time is your English class?"

   YOU ______________________________

3. "When are you free this week?"

   YOU ______________________________

LESSON 2

9 Choose the correct responses to complete the conversation. Write the letter on the line.

A: Excuse me. I'm looking for Palermo's.

B: ____ 1.

A: Yes. Is it around here?

B: ____ 2.

A: It's 610 Pine Street.

B: ____ 3.

A: Really? That's great. Thanks.

B: ____ 4.

a. Well, Pine Street is right around the corner.

b. I think it is. Do you know the address?

c. No problem.

d. Palermo's? The Italian restaurant?

10 Look at the pictures. Answer the questions.

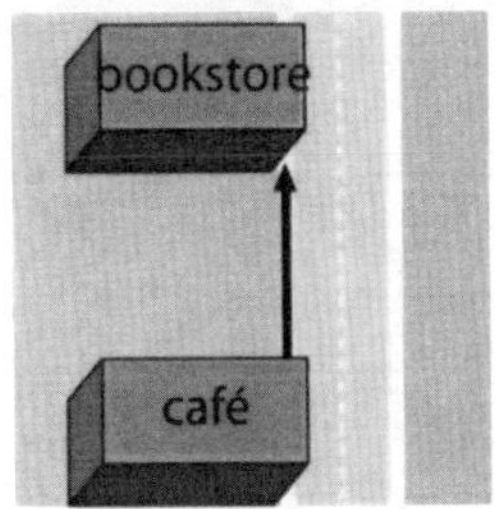

1. Where's the bookstore?

   It's down the street from the café.

2. Where's the theater?

   ____

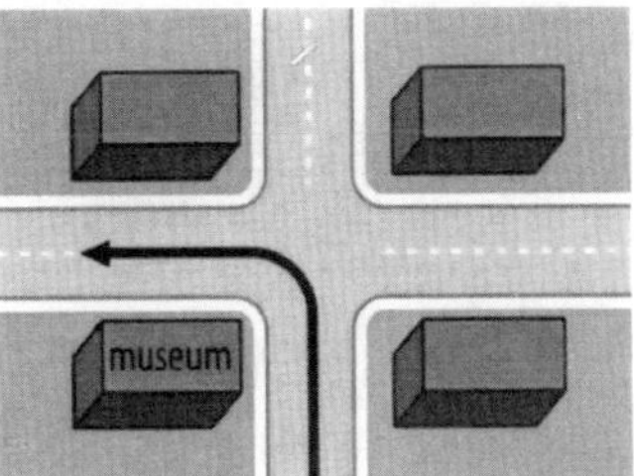

3. How do I get to the museum?

   ____

4. How do I get to the bank?

   ____

5. Where's the post office?

   ____

6. How do I get to the school?

   ____

11 **Look at the map. Answer the questions.**

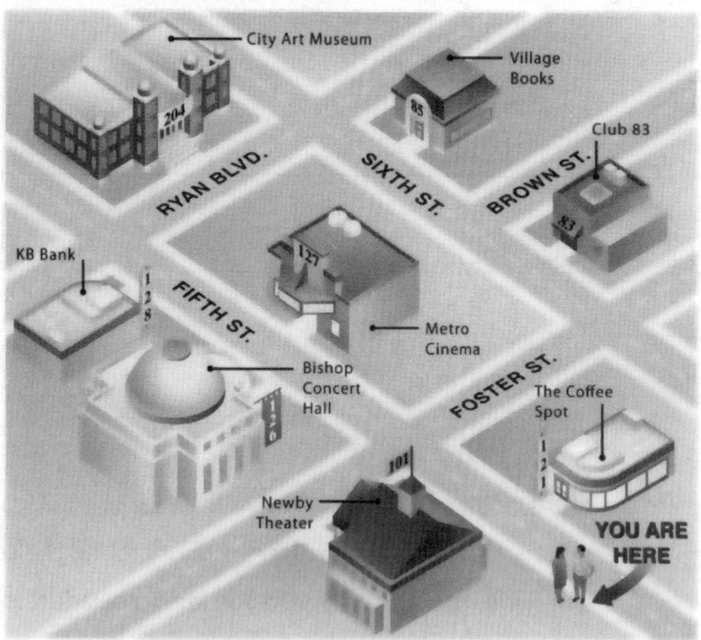

1. A: Where's the Metro Cinema?
   B: ______________________________
2. A: How do I get to the City Art Museum?
   B: ______________________________
3. A: Where's KB Bank?
   B: ______________________________
4. A: How do I get to the Newby Theater?
   B: ______________________________
5. A: Where's Club 83?
   B: ______________________________
6. A: How do I get to Village Books?
   B: ______________________________

12 CHALLENGE. **Write directions from your home to your school or a place in your community.**

Start at: ______________________ (your address)

Go: ______________________________

____

____

____

____

____

End at: ______________________ (address of final destination)

13 **Look at the festival events listing. Then answer the questions. Use in, on, or at, if possible.**

10th Annual Asian Folk Festival — Saturday, May 10 at the Park Arts Center in Rand Park — **Events Listing**

Time	Location	Event	
1:00 P.M.	Rand Park	Kite-Making Workshop	Children can make their own kite to fly in the park
3:00 P.M.	The Park Arts Theater	Japanese Play: Children's Kabuki Group	Watch middle school students from Kobe, Japan perform a traditional play
7:00 P.M.	The Rand Park Band Shell	Javanese Concert: Kiai Kanjeng Gamelan Orchestra	Hear music featuring drums, cymbals, and gongs from Java, Indonesia
6:00 P.M.	The Rand Park Band Shell	Korean Dance: "Bu-che Chum" Fan Dance Troupe	See colorful dancers from Suwon, Korea perform a beautiful fan dance
5:00 P.M. and 9:45 P.M.	The Park Arts Theater	Chinese Movie: *The Story of Lotus*	A love story set in the beautiful Wuyi mountains in Southern China

Plus try traditional Asian treats from China, Japan, Korea, and Indonesia. Food stalls will be open in the park from 12:00 to 8:00 P.M.

1. When's the Asian Folk Festival? ______
2. Where's the Japanese play? ______
3. What time is the Javanese concert? ______
4. Where's the Chinese movie? ______
5. What event is at 6:00 P.M.? ______

14 **Complete the instant messages with information from the Asian Folk Festival listing.**

Lara - Conversation

File Edit Actions Tools Help

Invite Send Files Webcam Audio Launch Site

To: **Lara** Lara@email.com

Peter says: Hi, Lara. Are you free on ______ (1.)?
Lara says: Yes. Why?
Peter says: The Asian Folk Festival is at the ______ (2.) in ______ (3.)
Lara says: What kind of festival?
Peter says: An Asian culture festival. Let's see . . . There's a Chinese movie, a Japanese ______ (4.), a Korean ______ (5.) and a Javanese ______ (6.)
Lara says: Really? Sounds like fun!
Peter says: I know you're a movie fan. Want to see the movie?
Lara says: OK. What time?
Peter says: There's an early show at ______ (7.) and a late show at 9:45.
Lara says: Let's go to the early show— 9:45 is past my bedtime

15 Extra reading comprehension

Read the interviews on page 22 of the Student's Book again. How would the people answer questions about their musical tastes? Check all correct answers.

Damir Rudic

Do you go to concerts?
◯ yes ◯ no

How do you listen to music?
◯ on CDs
◯ on the Internet
◯ on the radio
◯ on music videos
◯ on TV music channels
◯ on MP3s
◯ on cassettes

Moon-Jeong Curie Lim

Are you a music fan?
◯ yes ◯ no

What's your favorite kind of music?
◯ rock
◯ pop
◯ jazz
◯ R&B
◯ Latin
◯ classical
◯ folk
◯ rap / hip-hop

Adam Klagsbrun

Do you go to concerts?
◯ yes ◯ no

When do you listen to music?
◯ when I read
◯ when I drive
◯ when I work
◯ when I eat
◯ when I check e-mail
◯ all the time

16 Extra reading comprehension

Complete the statements with words from the box, based on information from the interviews on page 22 of the Student's Book.

live	classical	song	genre	MP3 player	channels

1. Alternative rock is Mr. Rudic's favorite music ____________.
2. Mr. Rudic enjoys the music ____________ on TV.
3. Ms. Lim listens to ____________ music to relax.
4. Ms. Lim buys songs on the Internet and downloads the files to her ____________.
5. Mr. Klagsbrun thinks CDs have better sound quality than ____________ music.
6. Mr. Klagsbrun downloads music, too. He pays one U.S. dollar per ____________.

17 **Read about the WOMAD festival. Then check true, false, or no information.**

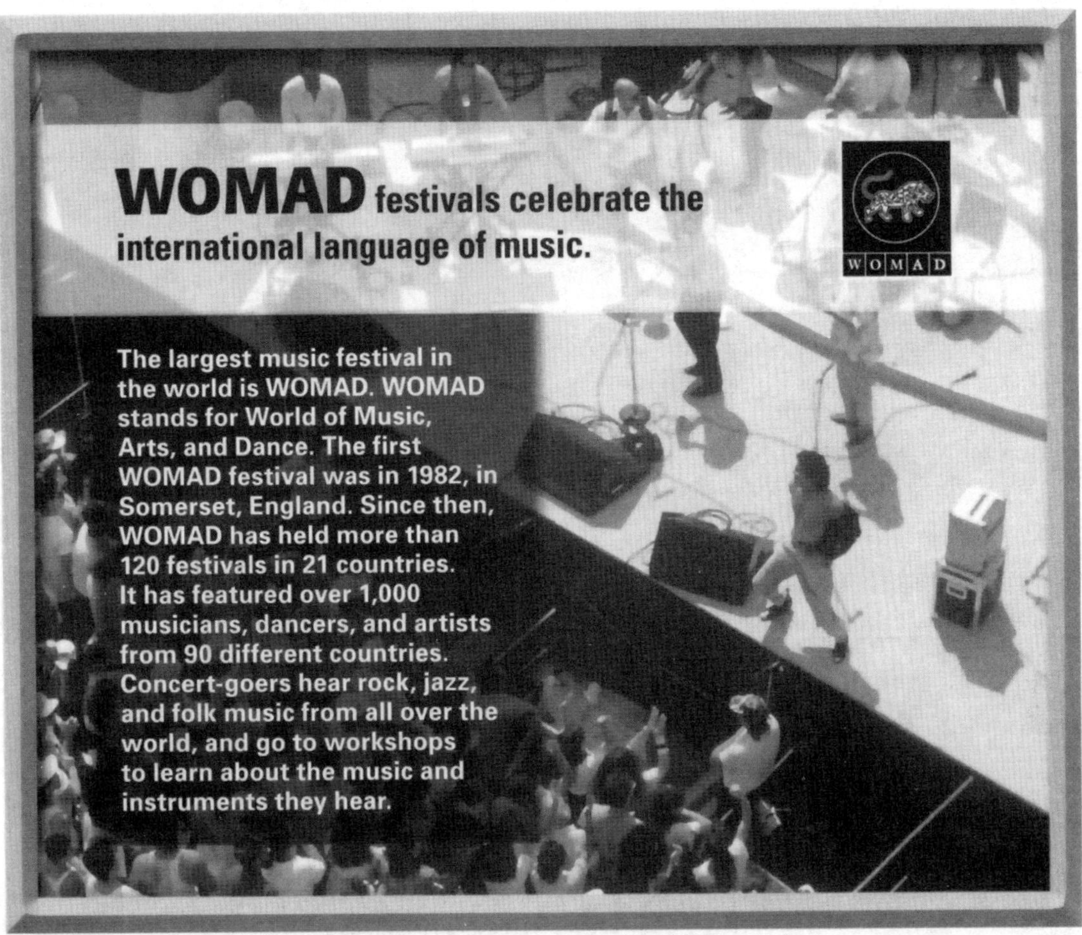

Source: www.womad.org

	true	false	no information
1. You can see a concert at the WOMAD festival.	☐	☐	☐
2. WOMAD is a classical music festival.	☐	☐	☐
3. WOMAD tickets cost $90.	☐	☐	☐
4. The musicians at WOMAD are from England.	☐	☐	☐

GRAMMAR BOOSTER

A **Complete the sentences. Write in, on, or at on the line.**

1. There are concerts _____ Saturday afternoons.
2. The bookstore is _____ my neighborhood.
3. My brother lives _____ Rome.
4. The lecture is _____ an art gallery.
5. I finish work _____ two hours.
6. I'm busy _____ the morning.
7. Chile is _____ South America.
8. My house is _____ Carmel Road.
9. The movie is over _____ midnight.
10. My parents got married _____ the 1960s.

B **Choose the correct answer. Circle the letter.**

1. "Where's the play?"
   a. At The Grand Theater. b. At 7:30. c. In the evening.
2. "What time is the movie in the park?"
   a. In March. b. Tomorrow. c. At dusk.
3. "When's the concert?"
   a. On Friday. b. On Ninth Avenue. c. At my school.
4. "What time is class?"
   a. In the evening. b. At 8:15. c. At the bank.
5. "Where's her meeting?"
   a. On Tuesday. b. At noon. c. At 44 South Street.
6. "When's the art exhibit?"
   a. In the center of town. b. In November. c. At the City Museum.
7. "What time's the talk?"
   a. September 21. b. Today. c. At 1 P.M.

Complete the event listings with prepositions of time and place. Write <u>in</u>, <u>at</u>, or <u>on</u>.

Arts Week

VOL 1.

Band Plans Free Concert

The Swingtime Jazz Band's first free concert is _at_ (1.) 8 P.M. ____ (2.) Monday. It's ____ (3.) Grand Hall ____ (4.) Wakefield Street ____ (5.) downtown Wellington. Call 999-555-8443 for more information.

Miracle Worker at Victoria University

Victoria University presents the play *The Miracle Worker* ____ (6.) 7:30 P.M. ____ (7.) Friday and Saturday, 4/23—4/24, and ____ (8.) 2:30 P.M. ____ (9.) April 25. The performances are ____ (10.) The Adam Concert Hall ____ (11.) Kelburn Road.

D **Complete the conversations. Write questions with When, Where, or What time. Complete the responses with a preposition.**

1. A: Where's the play ______________________?
   B: The play is __at__ The Landry Theater.
2. A: ______________________?
   B: I think the concert is ____ 8:30.
3. A: ______________________?
   B: The movie theater is ____ Park Road.
4. A: ______________________?
   B: The exhibit is ____ January and February.

E **Think of an event you'd love to go to. Answer the questions.**

1. What's the event?
   YOU ______________________
2. When's the event?
   YOU ______________________
3. What time's the event?
   YOU ______________________
4. Where's the event?
   YOU ______________________
5. Who can you invite?
   YOU ______________________
6. Pretend to invite someone. What do you say?
   YOU ______________________

WRITING BOOSTER

A **Circle the subject and underline the verb in each sentence.**

1. I love live music at jazz clubs.
2. U2 is a rock band from Dublin, Ireland.
3. Her parents aren't fans of hip-hop music.
4. *Mamma Mia!* is her favorite musical.
5. My husband listens to music on his commute.
6. They download music from the Internet.
7. Salsa music is fun to dance to.

B **Look at the music survey on page 23 of the Student's Book. Read the questions. Write your answers in complete sentences.**

1. Are you a music fan?

   YOU ______________________________

2. What's your favorite kind of music?

   YOU ______________________________

3. Who are your favorite artists?

   YOU ______________________________

4. When do you listen to music?

   YOU ______________________________

5. Do you go to concerts?

   YOU ______________________________

6. How do you listen to music?

   YOU ______________________________

7. How many CDs do you own?

   YOU ______________________________

Now circle the subject and underline the verb in each of your sentences. Check that each sentence begins with a capital letter and ends with a period.

C **Look at your notepad on page 23 of the Student's Book. On a separate sheet of paper, write at least five sentences about your partner and his / her tastes in music.**

UNIT 3

The Extended Family

Preview

1 **Complete the chart. Use the Vocabulary from page 26 of the Student's Book.**

Family relationships		
Words for males	**Words for females**	**Words for males and females**
son	daughter	children

2 **Complete the sentences with the correct family relationship.**

1. My sister's son is my ________________.
2. My mother's parents are my ________________.
3. My mother's brother's son is my ________________.
4. My sister's ________________ is my brother-in-law.
5. My brother's daughter is my ________________.
6. My wife's parents are my ________________.

3 **CHALLENGE. Look at the family tree website. Complete the sentences.**

1. Rita is a daughter-in-law, a wife, a sister-in-law, and a mother.
2. Jane is a ____________, a ____________, a ____________, and an ____________.
3. Evan is a ____________, a ____________, a ____________, and a ____________.
4. Mark is a ____________, a ____________, a ____________, and a ____________.

4 **Complete the sentences. Use words from the box.**

twins	adopted	an only child

1. My cousin Karen doesn't have any brothers or sisters. She's ______________.
2. Maddie and her brother Thomas were born on the same day. They're ______________.
3. Jake's mom and dad aren't his birth parents. He's ______________.

LESSON 1

5 **Match the words with similar meanings. Write the letter on the line.**

____ 1. divorced
____ 2. single
____ 3. married
____ 4. engaged
____ 5. separated
____ 6. widowed

a. married but not living together
b. ex-husband and ex-wife
c. planning to get married
d. not married
e. husband and wife
f. husband or wife dead

6 **Complete the sentences. Use live, have, or work in the simple present tense.**

1. She's married. She ______________ in an apartment with her husband.
2. He's single. He ______________ a wife.
3. My sister is separated. She ______________ a husband, but they ______________ in the same house.
4. She's engaged to her co-worker. She and her fiancé ______________ in the same office.
5. Kevin is divorced. His two children ______________ with his wife, but they visit him on weekends.

7 **Complete the paragraph. Use words from the box.**

likes	doesn't like	works	has
live	work	doesn't have	lives

Juanita Diaz ______________ (1.) in Puebla, Mexico. She ______________ (2.) in a restaurant. She ______________ (3.) Latin jazz, but she ______________ (4.) rock music. She's not really a rock fan. She ______________ (5.) any children, but she ______________ (6.) two nieces and one nephew. They ______________ (7.) in Tampico with Juanita's sister, Maria. Maria and her husband Roberto ______________ (8.) in a school.

8 Write yes / no questions and give short answers.

1. A: Do they live in New York?
   B: Yes, they do.
   (They live in New York.)
2. A: ______
   B: ______
   (Mr. Kelly has a large family.)
3. A: ______
   B: ______
   (They don't work in my building.)
4. A: ______
   B: ______
   (I speak English at work.)
5. A: ______
   B: ______
   (She lives with her parents.)
6. A: ______
   B: ______
   (We don't have any children.)
7. A: ______
   B: ______
   (My husband doesn't like show tunes.)
8. A: ______
   B: ______
   (I don't live with my fiancée.)

9 Choose the correct response to complete the conversation. Write the letter on the line.

A: ___ 1.
B: Actually, I have some good news and some bad news.
A: ___ 2.
B: My niece just got married.
A: ___ 3.
B: Thanks!
A: ___ 4.
B: My brother and sister-in-law just got separated.
A: ___ 5.

a. Really? That's fantastic.
b. What's new?
c. What's the good news?
d. Oh, no. I'm sorry to hear that.
e. What's the bad news?

10 Answer the questions. Use your own words.

1. "Do you live near your parents?"
   YOU ______
2. "Do you have any nieces or nephews?"
   YOU ______
3. "Do you work? What do you do?"
   YOU ______

LESSON 2

11 Read the information. Complete the statements.

Hi. My name is Brianna. My parents got divorced when I was very young. After a few years, my mother got married again. Her second husband's name is Ray. They have a daughter, Gabby. Gabby and I grew up together and we're very close. My father just got remarried. His new wife, Katherine, has two young boys, Jess and Avery. It's fun having two little brothers. They live nearby, so sometimes I baby-sit for them.

1. Brianna is Ray's ______.
2. Gabby is Brianna's ______.
3. Katherine is Brianna's ______.
4. Brianna is Jess and Avery's ______.
5. Brianna's father is Jess and Avery's ______.

12 Complete the questions with do or does.

1. Where ________ Aidan live?
2. When ________ you listen to music?
3. What ________ your half-brother do?
4. How often ________ you go to the movies?
5. What time ________ your husband go to work?
6. What ________ your friends call you?
7. How many brothers and sisters ________ you have?

13 Choose the correct response. Write the letter on the line.

____ 1. "What does Alex do?"
____ 2. "How many children does your sister have?"
____ 3. "Where does your mother live?"
____ 4. "How often do you call your stepsister?"
____ 5. "What time do you get home from work?"
____ 6. "When do you visit your grandmother?"
____ 7. "What do you and your husband do?"

a. In Madrid with my half-sister.
b. At 6:30.
c. He works at a bookstore.
d. We talk on the phone every day.
e. She has three.
f. On Sunday afternoons.
g. We're both teachers.

14 Look at the responses. Complete the questions.

1. A: What does Nick do?
   B: He's a computer programmer.
2. A: ________ your cousins ________?
   B: They live in Hong Kong.
3. A: ________ your mother ________ you?
   B: She visits me every year in May.
4. A: ________ concert tickets ________?
   B: I only have two.
5. A: ________ to school?
   B: We go at 8:30.
6. A: ________ a twin brother or sister?
   B: My friend Allison has a twin sister. Her name is Emma.

15 Write a paragraph about someone in your family. Use these questions for ideas.

- Who is it? What's his or her relationship to you?
- Where does he or she live?
- What does he or she do?
- Is he or she married or single?
- How many children (or brothers and sisters) does he or she have?
- How often / When do you see him or her?

LESSONS 3 and 4

16 Complete the sentences. Use words from the box.

same	kind	different	both	alike	similar

1. Robert and Peter wear dark suits to work. They wear the same ____________ of clothes.
2. Megan eats salads for lunch. Frank eats cheeseburgers and french fries. They like ____________ foods.
3. Elizabeth and her sister are identical twins. They look exactly ____________.
4. Mike likes rock, pop, and hip-hop music. Dave listens to rock and hip-hop. They like ____________ music.
5. My stepsister and I like the same music. We ____________ download show tunes and movie soundtracks.
6. Joe and Ryan both eat at this restaurant a lot. They like the ____________ food.

17 Look at the pictures. Complete the sentences.

1. Mary and Ida ____________ wear glasses.

2. Miki is a chef, ____________ Jamie isn't.

3. Antonio speaks English, but Yoko ____________.
4. Jim is a jazz fan, but Thomas ____________.

18 **Look at the questions and answers. Write sentences comparing the two people.**

	Jane	Mark
Do you like rock concerts?	yes	no
Do you have an MP3 player?	yes	yes

1. Jane likes rock concerts, but Mark doesn't.
2. Jane and Mark both have MP3 players.

	Chris	Lola
Do you like coffee?	yes	yes
Do you eat a big breakfast?	yes	no

3. ______________________________
4. ______________________________

	Mia	Rose
Do you have a large family?	yes	no
Do you live near your parents?	no	yes

5. ______________________________
6. ______________________________

	Joon	Sam
Are you a student?	yes	no
Do you work?	yes	yes

7. ______________________________
8. ______________________________

19 **Choose four relatives. Write each person's name, relationship to you, and one similarity or difference.**

1. Name: ______________ Relationship: ______________

   Similarity / Difference: ______________________________
   (Circle one.)

2. Name: ______________ Relationship: ______________

   Similarity / Difference: ______________________________
   (Circle one.)

3. Name: ______________ Relationship: ______________

   Similarity / Difference: ______________________________
   (Circle one.)

4. Name: ______________ Relationship: ______________

   Similarity / Difference: ______________________________
   (Circle one.)

20 **Read the article. Then complete the statements with words from the article.**

Blending Families: Advice for Stepparents

Blended families, or stepfamilies, are now very common. In the U.S., at least one-third of all children will be part of a blended family before they reach the age of eighteen. At first, the changes for children in blended families may be difficult. But most blended families are able to work out their problems and live together happily.

What is a blended family?

In a blended family, one or both parents have children from earlier relationships. The parents may be divorced or widowed. When they decide to get married again, they bring children from their first marriage to live with their new husband or wife and, in some cases, his or her children.

What can new stepparents do?

While the new marriage is exciting for the parents, the children may be worried. Will they have a good relationship with their new stepfather or stepmother? What will their new stepbrothers and stepsisters be like?

A few important things for new stepparents to remember are:

- Be realistic: Everything won't be perfect in the beginning.
- Be patient: Good relationships take time.
- Don't expect too much: Give your stepchildren your time, energy, and love, but don't expect anything in return for now.

The good news is that, with good communication and a lot of support, kids usually adjust to their new family members. The bad news? Creating a healthy blended family takes hard work and a lot of time.

Source: helpguide.org

1. Another name for a blended family is a __________.
2. About __________ of children in the U.S. live in blended families.
3. In a blended family, at least one parent has __________ from a previous marriage or relationship.
4. Children in a new blended family may feel __________.
5. Stepparents should be __________ and understand that it takes time to build good relationships.

21 Extra reading comprehension

Look at the website on page 34 of the Student's Book again. Circle the letter of the correct answer.

1. Who is the question from?
   - a. a daughter
   - b. a father
   - c. Mr. Dad
   - d. a mother
2. What do the parents want to do?
   - a. sell their house
   - b. send their last child off to college
   - c. travel
   - d. both a. and c.
3. Who doesn't have a job?
   - a. the father
   - b. the mother
   - c. Mr. Dad
   - d. the oldest daughter
4. According to the website, what do more adult children do today than in the past?
   - a. move out of the house
   - b. return home to live
   - c. get divorced
   - d. go off to college

22 Extra reading comprehension

Look at the website on page 34 of the Student's Book again. What advice does "Mr. Dad" offer to worried parents of adult children living at home? Write Do or Don't on the line.

______ 1. Worry.

______ 2. Help in any way you can.

______ 3. Ask, "How long do you plan on staying?"

______ 4. Treat your adult children like kids.

______ 5. Tell them you understand.

______ 6. Talk to them as adults.

______ 7. Discuss paying for expenses and helping with chores.

GRAMMAR BOOSTER

A Choose the correct response. Write the letter on the line.

____ 1. "Do you and your brothers play soccer together?"

____ 2. "Does your stepbrother work in a restaurant?"

____ 3. "Do your grandparents like music?"

____ 4. "Does your aunt look like your mother?"

____ 5. "Do you live near here?"

____ 6. "Do I need a tie?"

a. No, he doesn't.

b. Yes, we do. All the time.

c. No, I don't.

d. Yes, they do. Very much.

e. No, she doesn't.

f. No, you don't.

B Complete the conversations. Write short answers to the questions.

1. A: Does he live in Sydney?
   B: *No, he doesn't*. He lives in Melbourne.
2. A: Do your friends like Chinese food?
   B: ______. They go to Chinese restaurants all the time.
3. A: Do you have a big family?
   B: ______. I have eight brothers and sisters.
4. A: Does your husband work in an office?
   B: ______. He's a musician.
5. A: Do we need to buy our tickets now?
   B: ______. We can buy our tickets on the train.

C Complete the conversations. Write yes / no questions with the simple present tense.

1. A: He doesn't like concerts.
   B: *Does he like* art exhibits?
2. A: My sister-in-law doesn't eat meat.
   B: ______ fish?
3. A: My stepfather doesn't drink coffee.
   B: ______ tea?
4. A: I don't like rap music.
   B: ______ jazz?
5. A: I have two brothers and one sister.
   B: ______ any nieces and nephews?

D **Look at the responses. Write information questions with the simple present tense.**

1. A: How many people do you have in your office ?
   B: In my office? About twenty or twenty-five people.
2. A: ____?
   B: Max? He works in London.
3. A: ____?
   B: They usually start work at 8:00.
4. A: ____?
   B: My mother. She calls me every night.
5. A: ____?
   B: The Perez family lives here.
6. A: ____?
   B: Mona? She only has one sister.
7. A: ____?
   B: He sees his cousins every summer.

E **Read each statement. Underline the subject and circle the object. Write two questions with who, one about the subject and one about the object.**

1. My son visits my parents once a month.
   a. Who visits your parents once a month? My son.
   b. Who does your son visit once a month? My parents.
2. My grandmother lives with my aunt.
   a. ____? My grandmother.
   b. ____? My aunt.
3. Nathaniel loves Beethoven.
   a. ____? Nathaniel.
   b. ____? Beethoven.
4. Elliot works for Mr. Kim.
   a. ____? Elliot.
   b. ____? Mr. Kim.

How many people are there in the world? You can see a population clock on this website: www.census.gov/cgi-bin/ipc/popclockw

WRITING BOOSTER

Look at the sports website. Complete each sentence with and or but.

Ming vs. O'Neal

Back | Forward | Stop | Refresh

Address:

Yao Ming vs. Shaquille O'Neal

NICKNAME:
Ming Dynasty (USA), Little Giant (China)

HEIGHT:
7 feet, 6 inches / 2.29 m

WEIGHT:
310 pounds / 140.6 kg

DATE OF BIRTH:
September 12, 1980

NATIONALITY:
Chinese

HOMETOWN:
Shanghai, China

OCCUPATION:
athlete

FAMILY:
only child

MARITAL STATUS:
married, no children

MUSIC TASTE:
rap music, Chinese pop

NICKNAME:
Shaq, Superman

HEIGHT:
7 feet, 1 inch / 2.16 m

WEIGHT:
340 pounds / 154.2 kg

DATE OF BIRTH:
March 6, 1972

NATIONALITY:
American

HOMETOWN:
Newark, New Jersey, USA

OCCUPATION:
athlete, actor, musician

FAMILY:
two sisters and one brother

MARITAL STATUS:
married with three daughters, two sons, and one stepson

MUSIC TASTE:
rap music, R&B music

1. Yao Ming is tall, ____________ he's a basketball player.
2. Shaquille O'Neal is an athlete, ____________ he's an actor / musician.
3. Mr. O'Neal has two sisters and one brother, ____________ Mr. Yao is an only child.
4. Mr. Yao likes Chinese pop music, ____________ Mr. O'Neal doesn't.
5. Mr. O'Neal is married, ____________ he has six children.
6. Mr. Yao was born in the 80s, ____________ Mr. O'Neal was born in the 70s.

Look at the sports website again. On a separate sheet of paper, write a paragraph comparing Yao Ming and Shaquille O'Neal. Write about how they are similar and how they are different.

UNIT

4

Food and Restaurants

Preview

1 **Look at the menus. Then read the conversations. Where are the customers eating? Write the name of the restaurant on the line.**

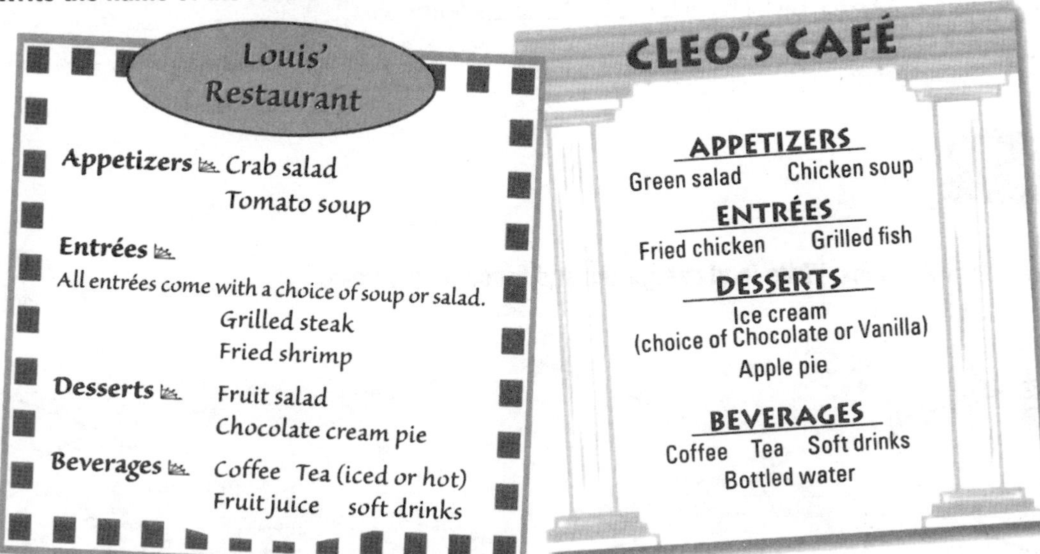

Louis' Restaurant

Appetizers Crab salad
Tomato soup

Entrées
All entrées come with a choice of soup or salad.
Grilled steak
Fried shrimp

Desserts Fruit salad
Chocolate cream pie

Beverages Coffee Tea (iced or hot)
Fruit juice soft drinks

CLEO'S CAFÉ

APPETIZERS
Green salad Chicken soup

ENTRÉES
Fried chicken Grilled fish

DESSERTS
Ice cream
(choice of Chocolate or Vanilla)
Apple pie

BEVERAGES
Coffee Tea Soft drinks
Bottled water

1. Cleo's Café

2. ______________

What comes with the entrées?

You have a choice of soup or salad.

3. ______________

Anything to drink?

Fruit juice, please.

4. ______________

2 **Look at the menus in Exercise 1 again. Where will you eat? What food will you order?**

I'll eat at ______________________. I'll start with the ______________________.
Then I'll have the ______________________. I'll have ______________________ to drink
and ______________________ for dessert.

Now change your mind about one dish your ordered.

On second thought, maybe I'll have the ______________ for ______________.

LESSON 1

3 **Complete the word webs. Write food categories and foods on the lines.**

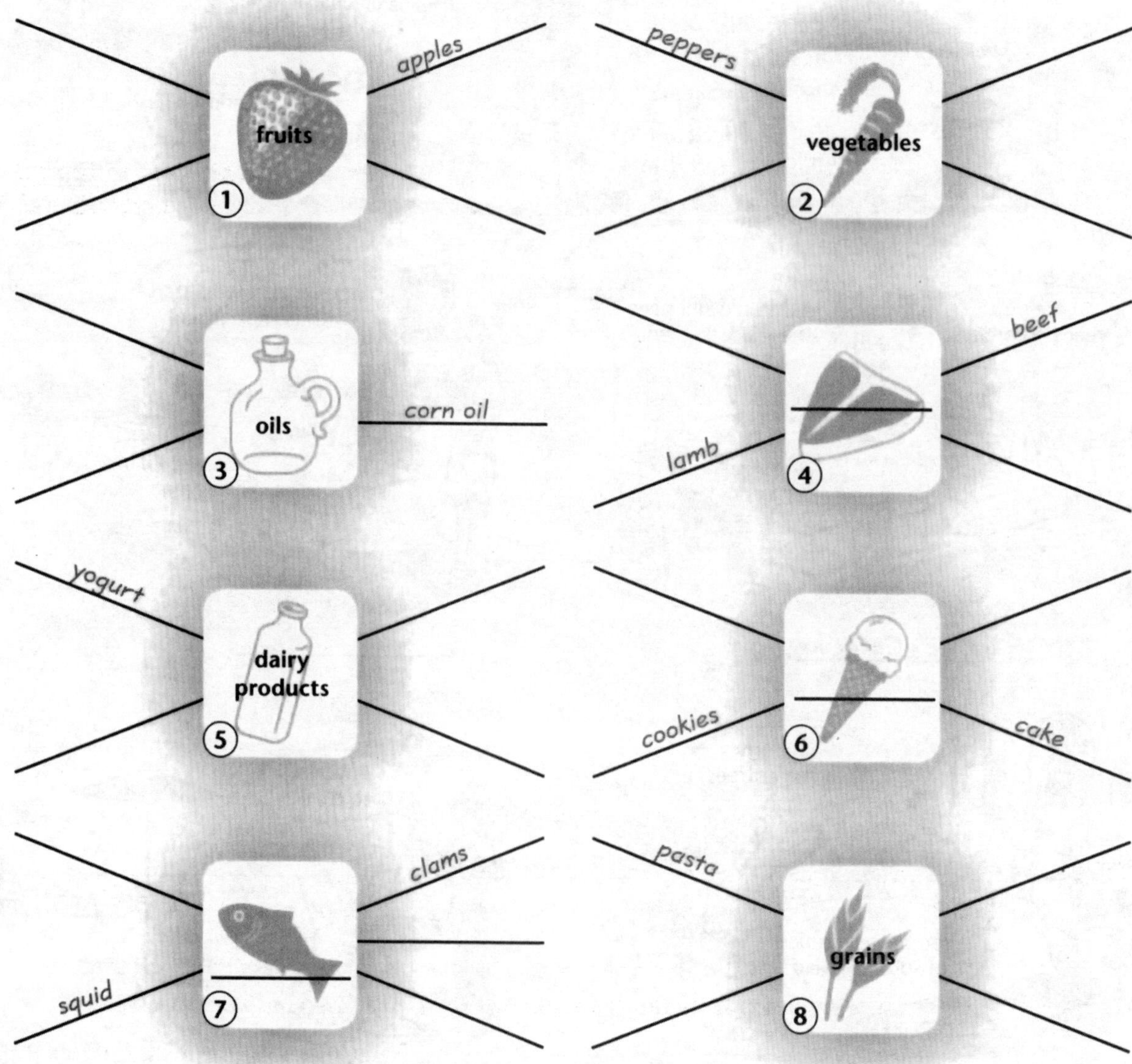

4 **What's in the fridge? Look at the picture. Write sentences starting with There is / There isn't or There are / There aren't.**

Non-count nouns	
fish	lettuce
sausage	juice
milk	broccoli
cheese	yogurt

Count nouns	
apple	carrot
banana	orange
egg	onion
grape	

5 **Think about your favorite dish at your favorite restaurant. What are the ingredients? Use There is / There are to write the ingredients you know. Use Is there / Are there to guess other ingredients.**

Dish: *Pad Thai* Restaurant: *Lemon Grass*
Location: *on the corner of First Avenue and Bank Street*
There's shrimp in the Pad Thai at Lemon Grass. Are there eggs?

Dish: Restaurant:
Location:

6 **Answer the questions. Use your own words.**

1. "Is there anything to eat in your fridge?"
   YOU ____________________
2. "How hungry are you right now?"
   YOU ____________________
3. "What restaurants in your area do you recommend?"
   YOU ____________________

LESSON 2

7 **Match the statement on the left with the explanation on the right. Draw a line.**

1. "All children's meals come with a drink and dessert."
2. "Does the grilled chicken come with a salad?"
3. "I think I'll start with the tomato soup."
4. "Anything to drink?"
5. "I need some more time."
6. "And what would you like for your main course?"

a. The customer is asking about the menu.

b. The server is explaining the menu.

c. The customer is not ready to order.

d. The server is taking a beverage order.

e. The customer is ordering an appetizer.

f. The server is taking the customer's entrée order.

8 **Complete the conversations.**

1. A: What do sandwiches ________________?
   B: Potato chips or fresh fruit.
2. A: What ________________ bread is there?
   B: White, wheat, or a croissant.
3. A: And anything ________________?
   B: Sparkling water, please.
4. A: Would you like to try our famous chocolate cake?
   B: No, thanks. I'm not in the ________________ dessert.

9 Complete the conversation with a, an, or the.

Mary: Let's get ____ (1.) table.

Joan: OK. Let's see. How about ____ (2.) table by the window? It's available.

Mary: Perfect.

Server: Are you ready to order?

Joan: Yes, we are. Do you have ____ (3.) breakfast special?

Server: Yes, we do. We have ____ (4.) Continental Breakfast Special and ____ (5.) English Breakfast Special on ____ (6.) menu today.

Joan: What does ____ (7.) Continental Breakfast Special come with?

Server: It comes with ____ (8.) choice of juice, tea, or coffee and ____ (9.) basket of fresh-baked French bread.

Joan: I think I'll have ____ (10.) English Breakfast Special with coffee, please.

Mary: I'll have the same, but without ____ (11.) coffee. I'll have ____ (12.) glass of juice instead.

Server: Certainly.

The Sunrise Café

Breakfast Specials:
All specials include your choice of coffee, tea, or juice.

Continental Breakfast:
Basket of fresh-baked French bread

English Breakfast:
Fried Eggs, Sausage, Tomatoes, Fried Potatoes

10 Complete the sentences with a, an, or the.

1. I'm in the mood for ____ cheeseburger.
2. ____ Caesar salad at Mario's is fantastic.
3. Is there ____ children's menu?
4. Would you like to start with ____ appetizer?
5. It's Elizabeth's birthday. Let's pick up ____ cake.
6. I recommend ____ curry chicken. It's delicious.
7. Are there eggs in ____ Chinese noodles?
8. For breakfast, I usually have coffee with milk and ____ banana.
9. ____ orange juice here is fresh-squeezed.

11 Answer the questions. Use your own words. Use a, an, or the if needed.

1. "Hungry? What are you in the mood for?"
   YOU ____
2. "What dish do you recommend at your favorite restaurant?"
   YOU ____
3. "What do you usually eat for breakfast?"
   YOU ____

LESSONS 3 and 4

12 **Look at the menu. Then answer the questions with short answers.**

1. Does the pasta come with a salad?
   Yes, it does.
2. What kind of soup is there?
   ____
3. Is there any seafood on the menu?
   ____
4. Are there any healthy foods on the menu?
   ____
5. Is the fish entrée spicy?
   ____
6. Does this restaurant accept credit cards?
   ____
7. What kind of salad is there?
   ____

JACK'S RESTAURANT

SOUPS
Clam Chowder Chicken Vegetable

SALADS
Pasta Salad Mixed Green Salad

ENTRÉES
ALL ENTRÉES INCLUDE A CHOICE OF SOUP OR SALAD.
Teriyaki Steak with mashed potatoes
Vegetable Beef Stew with carrots, potatoes, and peas
Pasta with tomato sauce
Grilled Fish with garlic and red pepper sauce

LITE ENTRÉES
Low-Fat Baked Chicken with cottage cheese and fresh fruit
Vegetable Sandwich—sweet bell peppers, cucumbers, carrots, and mixed salad greens on pita bread

BEVERAGES
Bottled Water Soft Drinks Tea Coffee

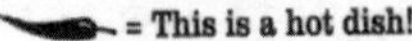 = This is a hot dish!

SORRY, WE DO NOT ACCEPT CREDIT CARDS.

13 

Read the webpage on page 46 of the Student's Book again. Circle the healthier fast-food options.

1. a. chicken b. red meat
2. a. grilled b. fried
3. a. sauce b. lettuce and tomato
4. a. regular-size portion b. super-size portion
5. a. french fries b. fruit cup or side salad
6. a. frozen yogurt or fruit ices b. ice cream or cookies

Now answer the questions, according to the website.

1. What's unhealthy about sauces?
   ____
2. What's healthy about tomato, lettuce, onion, and other veggies?
   ____
3. What's unhealthy about french fries?
   ____
4. What's healthy about frozen yogurt or fruit ices?
   ____

What will you order the next time you have fast food? Explain why.

14 **Create a menu for the Healthy Choice Café. Write healthful foods that you like to eat under each menu category.**

Healthy Choice Café

"EAT OUT WITH US AND EAT SMART!"

Appetizers

Raw veggie platter

Soups

Entrées

Desserts

Beverages

GRAMMAR BOOSTER

A **Complete the chart with nouns from the box.**

~~music~~	~~apple~~	water	fun	banana	cheese	help	egg
cookie	carrot	sugar	fruit	bread	golf	onion	coffee

COUNT	NON-COUNT
apple	music

B **Write How much or How many to complete the questions. Then answer each question, using a countable quantity. Use your own words.**

1. "________________ water do you drink in a day?"
   YOU ____

2. "________________ milk is in your refrigerator?"
   YOU ____

3. "________________ potato chips do you eat in a week?"
   YOU ____

4. "________________ bread do you buy every week?"
   YOU ____

5. "________________ onions do you use in a month?"
   YOU ____

6. "________________ sugar do you put in your coffee?"
   YOU ____

C **Complete the e-mail. Write a or an in front of count nouns or x in front of non-count nouns.**

Brad,

I need ____ (1.) help with dinner today. Can you go to the store and buy ____ (2.) liter of milk and ____ (3.) loaf of bread? We also need ____ (4.) onion or two, and ____ (5.) kilo of apples. Do you think we have ____ (6.) cheese? If not, please get ____ (7.) package of that, too. I'll see you at home after 5:00.

Tracy

D **Complete the conversations with some or any. For some items, more than one answer may be possible.**

1. **A:** Do you need __________ bread?
   B: No, thanks. I have __________.

2. **A:** Do they want __________ soup?
   B: No, they don't want __________ right now.

3. **A:** I don't have __________ water and I'm so thirsty.
   B: Do you want __________ tea?

4. **A:** Does she need __________ help?
   B: She doesn't need __________ help. She needs __________ practice.

WRITING BOOSTER

A **Connect the following words and ideas with and and in addition.**

1. Spanish paella is made with rice, seafood, meat, ________________ vegetables.
2. A traditional Irish breakfast includes sausages, bacon, ________________ fried eggs. ________________, there are fried potatoes and tomatoes.
3. Pho is a soup from North Vietnam, ________________ it's made with beef and rice noodles.
4. Guacamole is a Mexican appetizer made from avocados. ________________, it contains tomatoes, onions, lemon or lime juice, ________________ salt.
5. Indian samosas are fried pastries, ________________ they have a spicy filling of potatoes, peas, onions, ________________ green chilis.

B **Think of a typical dish from your country. Answer the questions.**

1. What is the name of the dish? ________________
2. What kind of dish is it (appetizer, entrée, side, etc.)? ________________
3. What region of your country is it from? ________________
4. What are the main ingredients? ________________
5. Is it spicy, salty, or sweet? ________________
6. Is it healthy? Why or why not? ________________

C **Write a paragraph describing the dish from Exercise B. Use and and in addition when possible.**

UNIT 5

Technology and You

Preview

1 **Look at the electronics on page 50 of the Student's Book. List the products in each category. Some products can be listed in more than one category.**

For listening to music	For watching movies	With your computer
headphones		
While driving	**While on vacation**	

2 **Complete the chart. Use electronic products from page 50 of the Student's Book.**

Products I have	Products I need / want	Products I can live without

3 **Now look at the Products I have column. Circle any products you'd like to replace. Then choose two products you circled. Explain why you're ready for an upgrade. Use the vocabulary and language from pages 50–51 of the Student's Book.**

I need a new desktop computer. My desktop is nine years old. The thing's . . .

1.

2.

LESSON 1

4 Choose the correct response. Circle the letter.

1. "I'm looking for a new cell phone. Do you have any suggestions?"
   a. What's wrong with it? b. Want to come along? c. How about a Global Mobile?
2. "What are you doing?"
   a. I'm looking for a camcorder. b. I'm ready for an upgrade. c. It's driving me crazy!
3. "I hear the new X-phone is awesome."
   a. Is it on the blink? b. Is it expensive? c. Is it a lemon?
4. "The photocopier isn't working."
   a. Are you online? b. Any suggestions? c. What's the problem?

5 Complete each conversation with the present continuous. Use contractions when possible.

6 **Read the questions. Write answers starting with No. Use the information in parentheses. Use contractions when possible.**

1. Is he leaving at 10:30? (11:00)
   No, he isn't. He's leaving at 11:00.
2. Are they studying at the library? (look at the newspaper ads)
   ____
3. Are you shopping for a laptop? (a smart phone)
   ____
4. Is she going to the movie tonight? (tomorrow night)
   ____

7 **Write questions starting with Is or Are.**

1. you / look for / a new fax machine
   Are you looking for a new fax machine?
2. he / check / e-mail / right now
   ____
3. they / buy / a scanner
   ____
4. Kate / work / today
   ____

8 **Look at the responses. Complete the questions. Use the present continuous.**

1. A: What *are you looking for*?
   B: I'm looking for a dictionary.
2. A: Who ______________________________?
   B: Matt is going to the tech conference.
3. A: What ______________________________?
   B: I'm buying a new mobile phone.
4. A: When ______________________________?
   B: My sister is going to Dublin in September.

9 **Look at Maria's smart phone. Answer the questions about her schedule. Use the present continuous. Use contractions when possible.**

1. It's 12:15 P.M. What is Maria doing?
   ____
2. It's 4:00 P.M. Is Maria going shopping?
   ____
   What is she looking for?
   ____
3. It's 9:15 P.M. Is Maria eating dinner?
   ____
   What is she doing?

10:00 A.M.
Call travel office

11:30 A.M.
Call Ed about movie

12:00 P.M.
Have lunch with Peter

4:00 P.M.
Shopping: Look for camcorder

7:00–8:30 P.M.
Have dinner with Mom and Dad

9:00 P.M.
See movie with Ed

10 Answer the questions. Use your own words.

1. "Are you using any electronic products right now?"

   YOU ______________________________

2. "What are you doing tonight?"

   YOU ______________________________

3. "What about next weekend?"

   YOU ______________________________

LESSON 2

11 Complete the conversation. Use questions from the box.

What's wrong with it?	How's it going?	Any suggestions?	What brand is it?

A: Hi, Barry. ______________________________ 1.

B: OK, thanks. But my coffee maker's driving me crazy!

A: Not again! ______________________________ 2.

B: I don't know. It just isn't working. That thing is a piece of junk!

A: That's too bad. ______________________________ 3.

B: It's a Coffee Pal.

A: Sounds like you need a new coffee maker.

B: That's for sure. ______________________________ 4.

A: Well, how about a Brewtech? The model I have is terrific.

B: Really? Thanks for the suggestion.

12 Complete the responses. Use words from the box.

hair dryer	blender	freezer	washing machine	fan	microwave

1. A: The juicer isn't working.
   B: Try the ____________________.
2. A: The chicken is still not done. This oven is so slow!
   B: Let's put it in the ____________________.
3. A: Are you ready to go to the Laundromat?
   B: Again? Too much trouble. I hear Appliance World is having a sale on ____________________s.
4. A: The air conditioner is on the blink again.
   B: Do we have a ____________________?
5. A: You look different.
   B: I look horrible! My ____________________ is broken! I'm going shopping for a new one at lunch.
6. A: Are we having these steaks tonight?
   B: No, they're for next week. Please put them in the ____________________.

13 Write each response in a different way.

1. A: What's wrong?
   B: My printer won't print.
   My printer's not working.
2. A: What do you think about Pell brand computers?
   B: Pell computers are great!
   ____
3. A: My TV isn't working. I can't watch the big game tonight.
   B: I'm sorry to hear that.
   ____
4. A: How's your new CD player?
   B: It's a piece of junk!
   ____

14 Answer the questions. Use your own words.

1. "Are you using any household appliances or machines right now?"
   YOU ______________________
2. "What household appliances and machines do you use every day?"
   YOU ______________________
3. "What household appliances and machines do you never use? Why?"
   YOU ______________________

LESSONS 3 and 4

15 Think about the features of products you have or know about. Write one product for each adjective. Explain your answers.

1. guaranteed: blender
   I can return it if I don't like it.
2. portable: ______________________
3. affordable: ______________________
4. obsolete: ______________________
5. popular: ______________________
6. convenient: ______________________

16 Extra reading comprehension

Read the advertisement on page 56 of the Student's Book again. Then check true, false, or no information.

	true	false	no information
1. You use your MP3 player with the Pro Musica.	☐	☐	☐
2. With the Pro Musica, you don't need a radio.	☐	☐	☐
3. Family members can listen to different music at the same time.	☐	☐	☐
4. The Pro Musica comes with CDs.	☐	☐	☐
5. You plug the speakers and earbuds into the Pro Musica.	☐	☐	☐
6. It's easy to download music onto the Pro Musica.	☐	☐	☐

17 **Read the article about a famous electronic product.**

Presenting the Sony, er . . . Stowaway?

Mr. Akio Morita and Mr. Masaru Ibuka started the Sony Corporation in Tokyo in 1946. At first, Sony was a small electrical repair company. In 1953, they started to sell the first transistor radios. In 1979, Sony introduced one of their most famous products, the "Walkman" portable cassette player.

Sony engineers invented the Walkman after they noticed young Japanese people listening to music all day, even carrying large stereos to the park. They believed that people wanted a music player that was small enough to wear in a shirt pocket. Sony also wanted the cassette player to be easy to use, so that people could listen to music while doing other things like exercising, riding the train, or doing housework.

Sony chose the name "Walkman" for their new product. At first, the Walkman didn't sell well. Electronic stores didn't think people would buy it. Some thought that the Walkman would make people unfriendly and stop talking to other people. However, as more people heard about the Walkman, it became a big hit. Japanese music fans loved it. When Sony was ready to sell the Walkman in other countries, they worried that people would think that the name was bad English. They made plans to call it the "Soundabout" in the United States and the "Stowaway" in the United Kingdom. But Mr. Morita wanted his gadget to have the same name in every country, and now "Walkman" is its name all over the world. You can even find "walkman" in the dictionary! Since 1979, there have been 300 different Walkman models and over 150 million have been sold around the world. Today's Walkman is a video MP3 player with built-in wireless Internet. The Sony Walkman is the best selling consumer electronic product ever made.

Sony Walkman ™ Cassette Player

SOURCE: www.sony.net

Now read the article again. According to the information in the article, which adjectives describe the Sony Walkman? For the adjectives you check, find words in the text to support your answers.

- ☑ convenient *easy to use, listen to music while doing other things*
- ☐ guaranteed ______
- ☐ affordable ______
- ☐ fast ______
- ☐ portable ______
- ☐ popular ______

Do you think that the Sony Walkman Cassette Player was a good product? Would you buy a new Walkman Player today? Explain your answers.

18 **Look at the picture. Then complete the paragraph. Use the present continuous.**

It's a busy Monday morning at the office of Techco Inc. The company president, Ms. Cline, _is answering_ (1. answer) her e-mail. She ________ (2. leave) tomorrow morning. She ________ (3. go) to Brazil for a sales meeting. Her assistant, Frank, ________ (4. talk) on the phone right now. He ________ (5. buy) Ms. Cline's airplane tickets. Jim, a sales manager, ________ (6. use) the photocopier and the fax machine. He ________ (7. make) copies of a report for the meeting and ________ (8. send) a fax to Ms. Cline's hotel. Jeff and Aliza also work for Techco. They ________ (9. clean) the break room and ________ (10. make) coffee.

19 **Look at the picture. Find all of the problems in the office. Write a short paragraph about the problems.**

The employees at Techno are having problems . . .

GRAMMAR BOOSTER

A **Change each statement from the simple present tense to the present continuous. Use contractions.**

1. I eat breakfast every morning. *I'm eating breakfast* ______ now.
2. My mother buys a newspaper every day. ______ now.
3. They walk to school every day. ______ now.
4. It rains all the time in the summer. ______ now.
5. He runs in the park every afternoon. ______ now.
6. We close the store at 5 P.M. ______ now.
7. He writes the report on Fridays. ______ now.

B **Write negative statements. Use the words in parentheses.**

1. He's going to school now. *He's not working.* ______. (work)
2. Sonia and Leo are drinking water. ______. (tea)
3. Ted is writing a letter. ______. (do homework)
4. You're talking a lot. ______. (listen)
5. I'm reading a magazine. ______. (a book)
6. We're eating at my house. ______. (a restaurant)
7. The fax machine is making a noise. ______. (print)

C **Choose the correct response. Write the letter on the line.**

____ 1. "Are you going to work now?"
____ 2. "Is he studying for an English test?"
____ 3. "What is Tina shopping for?"
____ 4. "Are they listening to jazz?"
____ 5. "When is he leaving work?"
____ 6. "Who's watching TV?"

a. A new rice cooker.
b. No, he's not.
c. Yes, I am.
d. In an hour.
e. Yuko and Miyumi.
f. No, they aren't. It's rap.

D **Unscramble the words to write questions. Use the present continuous.**

1. go / to the store / who *Who is going to the store?*
2. they / play soccer / where ____________________
3. Sam / eat / what ____________________
4. when / Lidia / come home ____________________
5. my computer / why / use / you ____________________
6. pay for / you / that / how much / laptop ____________________

WRITING BOOSTER

A **Rewrite the sentences. Use a form of have. Place the adjective before the noun.**

1. My GPS is new. *I have a new GPS.*
2. My food processor is convenient. ____________________
3. Our desktop computer is obsolete. ____________________
4. Her smart phone is awesome. ____________________
5. Their laptop is fast. ____________________
6. His video player is portable. ____________________

B **Write one sentence. Connect the adjectives with and.**

1. This camcorder is broken. It's also out-of-date.
   This camcorder is broken and out-of-date.
2. I hear Econotech scanners are good. They're affordable, too.
   ____
3. Microwaves are fast, and they are convenient.
   ____
4. These coffee makers are expensive, but they are guaranteed.
   ____
5. I'm looking for an up-to-date smart phone. And I'd like it to be small.
   ____

C **Look at the ad. Then write short answers to the questions.**

1. What is it? ______________________________
2. What brand is it? ______________________________
3. What model is it? ______________________________
4. What does it do? ______________________________
5. What adjectives describe it? ______________________________
6. Where do you use it? ______________________________
7. Is it a good product? Why or why not? ______________________________

D **Write a paragraph describing the product from Exercise C.**

About the Authors

Joan Saslow

Joan Saslow has taught in a variety of programs in South America and the United States. She is author of a number of multi-level integrated-skills courses for adults and young adults: *Ready to Go: Language, Lifeskills, and Civics; Workplace Plus: Living and Working in English;* and of *Literacy Plus*. She is also author of *English in Context: Reading Comprehension for Science and Technology.* Ms. Saslow was the series director of *True Colors* and *True Voices.* She participates in the English Language Specialist Program in the U.S. Department of State's Bureau of Educational and Cultural Affairs.

Allen Ascher

Allen Ascher has been a teacher and a teacher trainer in China and the United States and taught in the TESOL Certificate Program at the New School in New York. He was also academic director of the International English Language Institute at Hunter College. Mr. Ascher is author of the "Teaching Speaking" module of *Teacher Development Interactive*, an online multimedia teacher-training program, and of *Think about Editing: A Grammar Editing Guide for ESL.*

Both Ms. Saslow and Mr. Ascher are frequent and popular speakers at professional conferences and international gatherings of EFL and ESL teachers.

Authors' Acknowledgments

The authors are indebted to these reviewers who provided extensive and detailed feedback and suggestions for the second edition of *Top Notch* as well as the hundreds of teachers who participated in surveys and focus groups.

Manuel Aguilar Díaz, El Cultural Trujillo, Peru • **Manal Al Jordi,** Expression Training Company, Kuwait • **José Luis Ames Portocarrero,** El Cultural Arequipa, Peru • **Vanessa de Andrade,** CCBEU Inter Americano, Curitiba, Brazil • **Rossana Aragón Castro,** ICPNA Cusco, Peru • **Jennifer Ballesteros,** Universidad del Valle de México, Campus Tlalpan, Mexico City, Mexico • **Brad Bawtinheimer,** PROULEX, Guadalajara, Mexico • **Carolina Bermeo,** Universidad Central, Bogotá, Colombia • **Zulma Buitrago,** Universidad Pedagógica Nacional, Bogotá, Colombia • **Fabiola R. Cabello,** Idiomas Católica, Lima, Peru • **Emma Campo Collante,** Universidad Central Bogotá, Colombia • **Viviane de Cássia Santos Carlini,** Spectrum Line, Pouso Alegre, Brazil • **Fanny Castelo,** ICPNA Cusco, Peru • **José Luis Castro Moreno,** Universidad de León, Mexico • **Mei Chia-Hong,** Southern Taiwan University (STUT), Taiwan • **Guven Ciftci,** Faith University, Turkey • **Freddy Correa Montenegro,** Centro Colombo Americano, Cali, Colombia • **Alicia Craman de Carmand,** Idiomas Católica, Lima, Peru • **Jesús G. Díaz Osío,** Florida National College, Miami, USA • **Ruth Domínguez,** Universidad Central Bogotá, Colombia • **Roxana Echave,** El Cultural Arequipa, Peru • **Angélica Escobar Chávez,** Universidad de León, Mexico • **John Fieldeldy,** College of Engineering, Nihon University, Aizuwakamatsu-shi, Japan • **Herlinda Flores,** Centro de Idiomas Universidad Veracruzana, Mexico • **Claudia Franco,** Universidad Pedagógica Nacional, Colombia • **Andrea Fredricks,** Embassy CES, San Francisco, USA • **Chen-Chen Fu,** National Kaoshiung First Science Technology University, Taiwan • **María Irma Gallegos Peláez,** Universidad del Valle de México, Mexico City, Mexico • **Carolina García Carbajal,** El Cultural Arequipa, Peru • **Claudia Gavancho Terrazas,** ICPNA Cusco, Peru • **Adriana Gómez,** Centro Colombo Americano, Bogotá, Colombia • **Raphaël Goossens,** ICPNA Cusco, Peru • **Carlo Granados,** Universidad Central, Bogotá, Colombia • **Ralph Grayson,** Idiomas Católica, Lima, Peru • **Murat Gultekin,** Faith University, Turkey • **Monika Hennessey,** ICPNA Chiclayo, Peru • **Lidia Hernández Medina,** Universidad del Valle de México, Mexico City, Mexico • **Jesse Huang,** National Central University, Taiwan • **Eric Charles Jones,** Seoul University of Technology, South Korea • **Jun-Chen Kuo,** Tajen University, Taiwan • **Susan Krieger,** Embassy CES, San Francisco, USA • **Robert Labelle,** Centre for Training and Development, Dawson College, Canada • **Erin Lemaistre,** Chung-Ang University, South Korea • **Eleanor S. Leu,** Soochow University, Taiwan • **Yihui Li (Stella Li),** Fooyin University, Taiwan • **Chin-Fan Lin,** Shih Hsin University, Taiwan • **Linda Lin,** Tatung Institute of Technology, Taiwan • **Kristen Lindblom,** Embassy CES, San Francisco, USA • **Ricardo López,** PROULEX, Guadalajara, Mexico • **Neil Macleod,** Kansai Gaidai University, Osaka, Japan • **Robyn McMurray,** Pusan National University, South Korea • **Paula Medina,** London Language Institute, Canada • **María Teresa Meléndez de Elorreaga,** ICPNA Chiclayo, Peru • **Sandra Cecilia Mora Espejo,** Universidad del Valle de México, Campus Tlalpan, Mexico City, Mexico • **Ricardo Nausa,** Centro Colombo Americano, Bogotá, Colombia • **Tim Newfields,** Tokyo University Faculty of Economics, Tokyo, Japan • **Mónica Nomberto,** ICPNA Chiclayo, Peru • **Scarlett Ostojic,** Idiomas Católica, Lima, Peru • **Ana Cristina Ochoa,** CCBEU Inter Americano, Curitiba, Brazil • **Doralba Pérez,** Universidad Pedagógica Nacional, Bogotá, Colombia • **David Perez Montalvo,** ICPNA Cusco, Peru • **Wahrena Elizabeth Pfeister,** University of Suwon, South Korea • **Wayne Allen Pfeister,** University of Suwon, South Korea • **Cecilia Ponce de León,** ICPNA Cusco, Peru • **Andrea Rebonato,** CCBEU Inter Americano, Curitiba, Brazil • **Elizabeth Rodríguez López,** El Cultural Trujillo, Peru • **Olga Rodríguez Romero,** El Cultural Trujillo, Peru • **Timothy Samuelson,** BridgeEnglish, Denver, USA • **Enrique Sánchez Guzmán,** PROULEX, Guadalajara, Mexico • **Letícia Santos,** ICBEU Ibiá, Brazil • **Lyndsay Shaeffer,** Embassy CES, San Francisco, USA • **John Eric Sherman,** Hong Ik University, South Korea • **João Vitor Soares,** NACC, São Paulo, Brazil • **Elena Sudakova,** English Language Center, Kiev, Ukraine • **Richard Swingle,** Kansai Gaidai College, Osaka, Japan • **Sandrine Ting,** St. John's University, Taiwan • **Shu-Ping Tsai,** Fooyin University, Taiwan • **José Luis Urbina Hurtado,** Universidad de León, Mexico • **Monica Urteaga,** Idiomas Católica, Lima, Peru • **Juan Carlos Villafuerte,** ICPNA Cusco, Peru • **Dr. Wen-hsien Yang,** National Kaohsiung Hospitality College, Kaohsiung, Taiwan • **Holger Zamora,** ICPNA Cusco, Peru.